WHEN I WAS RED CLAY

WHEN I WAS RED CLAY

A JOURNEY OF IDENTITY, HEALING, AND WONDER

Jonathan T. Bailey

TORREY HOUSE PRESS

Salt Lake City • Torrey

First Torrey House Press Edition, August 2022
Copyright © 2022 by Jonathan T. Bailey

Published by Torrey House Press
Salt Lake City, Utah
www.torreyhouse.org

International Standard Book Number: 978-1-948814-63-8
E-book ISBN: 978-1-948814-64-5
Library of Congress Control Number: 2021941428

Cover art by Jonathan T. Bailey
Cover design by Kathleen Metcalf
Interior design by Rachel Buck-Cockayne
Distributed to the trade by Consortium Book Sales and Distribution

Torrey House Press offices in Salt Lake City sit on the homelands of Ute, Goshute, Shoshone, and Paiute nations. Offices in Torrey are on the homelands of Southern Paiute, Ute, and Navajo nations.

To the hummingbird I watched in her nest of spiderwebs and moss, babies warm against her blotched-green belly feathers. The Aztecs believed that successful warriors were quauhteca *who carried the sun before their reincarnation as hummingbirds. For their children, mothers are made of war and light.*

Contents

This book is a memory, which the Merriam-Webster dictionary defines as "the power or process of reproducing or recalling what has been learned and retained especially through associative mechanisms." Like memory, it is not linear, and does not begin, nor end, but exists as it emerged in dreams, journals, letters, poems, and thoughts—giving allowance for neurodivergent ways of experiencing the world. It is also a story of loss, and healing. For LGBTQ+ individuals throughout the world, the decision to come out is not easy, nor is it without consequences.

In the wake of loss, we pick up our brushes, our sewing needles, our microphones, and our pens, and we create a better world, regardless of whether we can inhabit it. We make loving families, and open-armed communities. In literature and art, we create new worlds where being different is not only tolerated but celebrated. Little by little, we lay nourishing soils where we once knew hardpan and plant seeds of inclusivity in our lives and for generations to follow.

The hand-painted cover of this book pays homage to the many gender, romantic, and sexual minorities who have explored their faith by tarot after being rejected by conventional religions. It is inspired by the 1909 Rider–Waite tarot card, the Moon. In poet and mystic A. E. Waite's book, *The Pictorial Key to the Tarot*, the Moon card represents "fears of the natural mind in the presence of that place of exit" and "calm upon [our] animal nature, while the abyss beneath shall cease from giving up a form." While tarot is a spiritual expression of which I don't partake, it is my honor to share this important part of gay culture, with its hard-won history of sacrifice and reconciliation.

If you walk away from this book with nothing else, I hope it is the value you find in yourself, in our communities, and the value we share in wild places. If you are struggling, please consult with the National Suicide Prevention Lifeline at 1-800-273-8255 and a mental health professional.

In solidarity,

Jonathan

foreword

Much like the dramatic landscapes and species that epitomize the North American deserts, Jonathan T. Bailey was wrought by formidable and unrelenting forces and elements into a unique and understated scholar and artist. The landscape and its inhabitants (past and present) are a personal sounding board that helps many of us naturalists navigate the elements of our personal, familial, and societal landscapes. A fortification against the fickle vagaries, and lingering side effects, of the Anthropocene.

Connecting with this young and sensitive autodidact has been a welcome turn of events—enhancing each other's understandings of the world from our unique backgrounds and experiences. Vibrant in Jonathan's work is a keen awareness inherent in Indigenous and ecologically minded people of "traditional ecological knowledge." That is, the kin-centric network of ever-extending relations—gardens of cognition—we all participate in. His dedication to conveying the beauty of rock art and desert landscapes has placed him close to "the mirror of nature." O'odham elder Camillus Lopez warns us that if we don't see ourselves in this mirror, we're standing too far away.

What you hold in your hands is a personal reflection and statement about healing and restoration across heart, mind, body, landscape, and species. In this current age we are faced with a specter of rapid change and uncertainty. Jonathan's works help us better manage how we deal with the lemons that life presents. If not lemonade, *something*. Think about the experiences and events that have brought you in meaningful touch with Earth and their inhabitants, and then back to yourself. Hold it, lean into it, learn from it, cherish it.

Robert A. Villa is a Tucsonan and naturalist deeply in love with the Sonoran Desert region. He currently presides over the Tucson Herpetological Society and is a research associate with the Desert Laboratory on Tumamoc Hill.

There is a box in red paper, exquisitely wrapped, tied with ribbon in eggshell blue. In the house, newscasters discuss school closures and downed power lines. The outline of an SUV vanishes at the end of my street. Visibility has gone to shit, and I have been far too distracted by thoughts of Mexican jays to shovel my driveway. A thermometer against the doorframe zeros out. I tap it with my fingernail, expecting it to climb to a reasonable temperature. It does not. I am one butt-fall away from packing my bags and moving south. The birds must've known what they were doing. I find no deliverer, no carolers, no solicitors. Just a box on a dreary December evening, a signal of goodwill, or perhaps a letter asking me to please stop wearing heels in public, signed with the fervent wishes of all of Utah. On its top is a card with fat cartoon sheep waddling over tinseled text that reads: Fleece Navidad.

It is a gift from my brother.

I peel off the paper slowly, anxious to preserve his origami handiwork; his obsession for a straight fold knew no bounds. Yet, I feel unjustifiably tense, as if it will reveal a secret buried deep in our genealogical record, or lift the lid of Pandora's box. The gift is heavy with something other than weight. Its gravity, I feel in my chest.

Inside, I find a disk with a handwritten label. The word *Family* is inscribed in fine-tipped marker. The DVD player turns on and I am met with seven hours of family movies: Christmases, birthdays, the time a skunk was caught in our tent while my father, expecting a late-night murderer, approached frantic-eyed, waving his imaginary finger gun. I watch for hours—every movie: my own, my siblings, my paternal grandparents who passed before they could register in the cumulus of human memory. But there is an omission, a word that does not cross our lips. It is a sound like wind through saguaro spines. You can hear it, feel it even, but it is mostly ineffable.

I was old, too old, when I first heard the word. Gay? Whatever it meant, I knew it was code for something undesirable. Televisions were shut off. Shouting drowned out unauthorized scenes in movies. We were pulled away from anything that did not evoke the Holy Ghost, a metaphysical personage guided by feelings, doctrine, and our gut intuition. In this house and community, one lesson cut through to me more than the others: gays were hated by God.

We lived in what some might call a rural bubble: a town of about a thousand residents, more livestock than people, and vagabond dogs townsfolk assured me would not bite. This was an untruth. Most of the streets were wider than necessary—no sidewalks, overgrown weeds, a few tall trees spilled into a picturesque pastiche of farms and fields. Here, beyond the reach of 1990s progress, people rarely left, and few arrived. With them, ideas of diversity and acceptance evaporated into rumors of a rapidly evolving (read: devilishly tempted) world.

Isolation was essential to preserving unadulterated faith in the teachings of the Church—the Church of Jesus Christ of Latter-day Saints, more commonly known as the Mormon Church—a religious institution shaped by the teachings and translations of Joseph Smith in 1830s New York. In our household, the list of prohibitions was long: tea, coffee, late-night cartoons, most video games, and media that might subject us to the effeminately inclined unmentionables. This was not a spoken rule, as speaking would bring truth to that three-letter word invoking unspeakable temptation, *gay*, but my understanding was carved deeply in pregnant silence.

As an official within the Mormon Church and a member of the priesthood, my father was given the "power and authority of God," evidenced by a vial of olive oil he clutched in his vest pocket. He placed the consecrated oil on the heads of the sick, or those needing to be blessed, or initiates into various roles within the church. With a drop, he invoked the power and authority of the Lord, the room cloaked in a suffocating musk of cologne as we dipped our heads in prayer.

Questioning my father was tantamount to questioning God. If he placed his faith against people who identified as gay, who was I to question him?

—

When my father wasn't fulfilling his duties to the church, or working at the region's coal-fired power plant, we traveled to the canyons of Utah's San Rafael Swell, hiking thousands of miles in landscapes that could rival any national park. Over time, I found words to describe its feast of color: forget-me-not blue, patina red-blue, sea-foam white, and arid yellow—a shade that could only be evoked by desert wildflowers. And then there was Navajo Sandstone, off-white by definition, but tempted by atmospheric color, like the deep azure of nightfall. When I was small, I believed this was a landscape malleable to tall tales and fictitious murmurations. It changed people, and they could, in turn, change *it*. All you needed was faith the size of a mustard seed, as we were told during sacrament testimonies, and mountains would move quite literally by our command. It made sense, then, that this was a setting for other worlds—the planet Vulcan of *Star Trek*, and a place where researchers simulated Mars-like conditions. It was a space on earth that represented but a sliver of God's power and, by extension, my potential under his glory. When a church official took me to the foothills of the Wasatch

Mountains and ordered me to move them with faith, wilderness became two things: a vessel for the church's authority and a symbol of my inherent unworthiness.

—

At 4:15 in the morning, my father nudged me awake, stuffing our bags in the truck while I rubbed my eyes and stumbled out to the front porch. Beyond our house were farms and ramshackle homesteads, a few more neighbors spread out with white-picket-fence properties, stately pines, and feral cats swatting mice in crop fields. At night, great horned owls emerged from roosts tucked within Douglas firs, joining in song with their mate, commencing a lovingly macabre ceremony by bobbing their heads in circular motions. Birders poetically describe this breeding window as "duet season" to reflect the melodic pairing that soon gives way to newly hatched owlets. In my hometown, breeding season was brief and intense, a period where big shadows moved between canopies without a feather disclosing their bodies. Once settled out of view, their booming, throaty music cut through with the intensity of Beethoven's fifth and I'd imagine that I somehow had found my place in the world. I belonged *here*, in the shadows between mountain and desert, where darkness and beauty exist like symbiotic mates. I believed myself kin to these owls, the coyotes, and the vultures. The unwanted, but inseparable from this place.

Once things were packed, we drove as the sun rose, passing the township of Moore, which I bequeathed the unloving title of Less. Population: five. Once a hotspot for arriving Mormon pioneers, the community was now reduced to wooden planks and pitched roofs, testimony to the stories of ancestors guarded in leather-bound dramas like family jewels. I, however, cherished this community for its other storied inhabitants: coyotes. My family never saw them, and I never wanted them to know. They were my little road trip secret, safe from bounty hunters and unspooling community gossip. Their outlines bobbed and weaved through the vegetation before cowering beneath the brambles, fiery white eyes gleaming through.

The highway soon entered badlands, and the badlands poured into sandstone canyons. The Swell opened to a devilish splendor of sparse vegetation, little water, and rolling cliffs of white sandstone. Early Mormon settlers came to these places and gave them names befitting their stark beauty: Devil's Canyon, Dead Man Canyon, Ghost Rock. *This was the place* for early pioneers: a tough and unforgiving landscape. A place, it may have seemed, to protect them from outside persuasion, or to keep the inside in. One morning, more cognizant than others, I wrote a poem here, unsure whether it recalled the juxtaposition of shadows, or the burn of something deeper within myself.

In the fall of a monarchy,
shadows relinquish,
no longer bowing
in moonlight.

In the fall of democracy,
rattlesnakes lie
on road's edge,
no longer swimming
through badland shadows.

In the rise of equity,
this lightness,
a filling drink
of moonlit waters,
slowly shifting.

We made our way to the canyons, packing our botas insulated with deer skin before descending into the backcountry. We soon came upon ancient images carved from deep purple walls of iron and manganese oxides, and I was endlessly fascinated. I dreamed vividly of rock art, almost lived more in the desert than at home, and spent every dime I could scrape on archaeological literature, twirling my fingers around the spines traced with titles like *Basketmaker Caves of Northeastern Arizona* or *The Serpent and the Sacred Fire*. When the great recession hit near my birthday, knowing our budget was worn thin, I asked only to visit a place I had loved very much. My parents were kind enough to buy me a fresh pair of books anyway, sliding them into my bag as we walked into the canyons, ready to indulge in their vast and indomitable presence.

—

I entered public school and my otherness was palpable. I was unsure whether it was my growing personal conflicts or my time in wilderness that other students so easily discerned. I became isolated in a new and scary way, often deciding the sub-zero temperatures outside were better than the hallways where I might be seen, noticed, or met with swinging fists.

I found a gap formed at the corner of the southwest walls of the school. If I huddled in this space with my back toward the field, I could avoid the frigid winter winds, however temporarily. I had a bad habit of showing up to school in a T-shirt and shorts, partly because I was a heavy kid who felt even larger in jeans, but mostly because the fabric caused me great sensory discomfort. I cinched my body close to my core, delaying the inevitable frostbite from reaching my extremities. Everything burned like hell. On particularly bad days, when taunting turned to assault, I fled school entirely, faking my absence with forged letters from my parents explaining that my grandfather had died, yet again. I left through chain-link gates raised at the entrance, acting out the daring escapes of popular nineties films.

One of my favorite places to visit followed the trajectory

of Ferron Creek, named after surveyor Augustus Ferron. Ferron descended upon the territory under the Homestead Act of 1862—which bequeathed 160 acres of public lands to ambitious individuals in exchange for the expansion of settlements in newly acquired western territories after the Mexican-American War. Ferron is said to have bargained naming rights for a dunking in the creek. Later, after being colonized by incoming Mormons, the town of Ferron—my hometown—was named after the creek.

The area was now bordered by verdant farmlands and the creek diminished to ephemeral pools of gray-green water—a consequence of the Millsite Dam upstream. In the summer months, snowdrifts high in the Wasatch Mountains begin to melt, pouring rapidly down into a reservoir many miles below. Excess water—a rare commodity in these haunts—releases through a spillway as if through a trapdoor. Oversupplied snowmelt wends its way back here to Ferron Creek, bringing life back to this ancestral drainage.

After ditching class, I walked along its polished river cobble, sometimes stripping off my shoes to feel the inundation of distant floods beneath my skin, twisting and turning my toes around jagged places where rock once resisted forces much larger than itself. On either side, the creek was surrounded by towering cottonwoods where mule deer gathered, feeding on fields of alfalfa in the outskirts of town.

In a few miles, low gray mesas appeared in thin, pale strokes on the horizon. On my hands and knees, I often worked my way to the tops of these geological wonders, making note of ancient architectural features and mounds of Mormon tea that so abundantly scattered the mesas. The plant's namesake beverage—Mormon tea—is prepared by boiling its long, green stems in water. Drinking the beverage can be an initiatory experience for Mormon youth, despite doctrine that now prohibits its consumption. I still remember my father filling his thermos, passing down ephedra tea for me to sip, his upper lip already outlined in a vermillion mustache. The most devout might argue this to be the root of my severe tea addiction, or at least they would if I didn't hide my chamomile like hard drugs.

Mormon tea is a plant within the genus *Ephedra*. The tea could be described as vanilla-like, albeit potentially toxic.* Early Mormon settlers found the plant to contain curative properties useful in the treatment of various ailments—likely with the uncredited help of neighboring Native American people—giving us its common names: Mormon tea and Brigham tea (after the early Mormon prophet, Brigham Young). As the genus *Ephedra* implies, the plant contains the chemical ephedrine, which was widely used by the public as a stimulant, decongestant, bronchodilator, and in the treatment of hypertension until it was banned with exceptions in 2004, after deaths and adverse reactions related to high dosages.

In the mesas, *Ephedra* would bloom around late May, producing plumes of sunny-colored flowers I looked forward to seeing every year, contrasted against the region's dull gray shale. Below these places, one could watch the humdrum of lumbering cattle grazing the fields surrounding a ranch house or two, their mouths brimming with half-chewed cud.

Henry David Thoreau once wrote, "in wildness is the salvation of the world." In these deserts, I found wilderness to be the salvation of the soul.

—

I was thirteen when I put the name with the feeling. I was gay. I did not want to be gay. It was just an attraction and I believed it to be changeable. In the words of apostle and leading authority in the Mormon Church, Boyd K. Packer:

There is a falsehood that some are born with an attraction to their own kind, with nothing they can do about

* Mormon doctrine prohibits the consumption of tea and coffee. It is unclear to me how brewing this plant was—and is—reconciled.

it. They are just "that way" and can only yield to those desires. That is a malicious and destructive lie. While it is a convincing idea to some, it is of the devil. No one is locked into that kind of life. From our premortal life we were directed into a physical body. There is no mismatching of bodies and spirits. Boys are to become men—masculine, manly men—ultimately to become husbands and fathers. No one is predestined to a perverted use of these powers.

Around this time, I became aware of conversion therapy at Brigham Young University, a private education institution owned by the Mormon Church. The process, it was said, would involve painful electrical shocks by attaching electrodes to sensitive areas like the armpits, chest, or penis. By having people view same-sex individuals in a state of undress while under extreme physical and psychological distress, the researchers believed they could create a repulsion for so-called homosexual tendencies. Three participants hanged themselves on the BYU campus in the aftermath of these experiments.

It was not long before I discovered that the program was shuttered during the 1970s after its apparent lack of success. Deprived of options, my stomach sunk. The life I had imagined—a wife, kids, being an example of goodness and faith—was gone. I lost sense of who I was, or why I even existed. Forced to reckon with my identity without faith, I grieved deeply. It is one thing to become estranged from the church, another to feel separated from your family, but the pain is at its worst when you are at war with yourself—when you feel as if you are not a sinner but the sin itself.

I climbed into the crawl-out space beneath my parent's house, an area once planned to be a lower expansion of the basement. Now, it was a lightless storage room carved from the earth, defined by walls of firmly packed soil. Old camping gear and retired Christmas decorations spread over the floor, coated in layers of dust and cobwebs. In the corners, curios from our childhoods were placed in boxes: old toys, photo albums, Halloween costumes a few sizes too small. A single red chair was propped against the entry, providing a foothold in the cavity where stairs were once planned. Tattered from decades of children planting their feet into the soft fabric, the chair was now an empty memory of my four siblings who had long since moved off to college. Alone and lulled by the hum of a washing machine that rattled from the floor above, I fell to the ground and wept.

—

Growing up in the church, we were taught that all defects were relieved in the afterlife, including sexual orientation. The choice was clear: to maintain an image of faith and virtue, and to prevent a lifetime of isolation and suffering, I should end my life. Though, I did not wish to cause trauma to those close to me. I wished to vanish. I wished to go quietly. Unable to complete the act on my own, I resorted to prayer, thinking a merciful God would end my life on my behalf. An act of compassion, I thought.

One afternoon, not long after my sixteenth birthday, a group of students caught me in the hallways of my high school. Loading an imaginary rifle and aiming it towards my head, they said they would kill me and that they had made plans to do so. To make a demonstration of their religious values, they vowed to finish the job by defecating on my corpse and dismembering my limbs. They pulled back on the fictitious trigger, recoiling from the explosion, or perhaps from the weight of their own conscience. A tragic exhibition of such intense hatred played out in late 2021, when a newlywed lesbian couple was murdered in similar manner in Moab, Utah, about a hundred miles from my hometown. Days later, apostle Jeffrey Holland encouraged members to pick up their metaphorical muskets to defend the church-owned Brigham Young University from the influence of LGBTQ+ allies.

In my school, shortly after threatening my life, students began exposing knives and firearms that they smuggled into class, quickly stuffing them back into their bags when noticed, their faces contorted in rabid grins of pride and vindication. There were times, times of deep and troubled contemplation, when I wondered if this was God's twisted way of answering my prayers.

After I reported the incidents to school officials, the situation only got worse. Some teachers made a solemn promise not to support "homosexual behavior" in any capacity. One went so far as to assign mandatory assignments to choose women from magazines that I "found attractive" and could "imagine [myself] marrying in the church," docking my grade if I refused to participate. Other teachers were supportive but hindered by Utah's so-called No Promo Homo law that prohibited teachers from speaking positively about gay people, which could cost them their employment if their protection was perceived as an endorsement of homosexuality.

When facing death, I became cognizant of the things I would lose. I mourned the desert deeply. I mourned my family. I acknowledged if death meant losing what I cherished most, it was no escape at all. I decided to drop out of high school and rescind my membership to the church.

—

When we were younger, we were taught that Mormonism was like a mirror, a perfect reflection of the heavens. Other religions, they would say, are a fractured portrayal of this mirror, each scavenging for a fragment of glass, a thin image of truth, shining a dull light upon their unfulfilled followers. What I have found is that, like a mirror, Mormonism presents only the image of yourself, but that image is backwards.

Once broken, once you have found the strength to leave, the mirror lies in a dust of powdered glass. You prowl the floors for a sliver, a shard, a reminder of your former self that now flows through your fingertips like fine grains of desert sand. It is only time and honesty that will give you back your personhood.

—

After leaving Mormonism, I did not find God in temples, nor in the church that topped the grassy hill a few minutes from my parents' house. In fact, I did not find God at all. I found something more profound in soil, with my hands pressed against the earth, feeling the journey of ancient roots. I sensed a powerful spirit when walking among bristlecone pines, surviving for thousands of years in rocky and inhospitable soils, their polished silver branches poised upwards as if to confirm their divine presence. In these spaces, aloneness is not isolation but incorporation, an enduring connection to our birth world. My testimony is no longer spoken behind a podium, but lost to the stirrings of wind, upholding the beating wings of canyon wrens.

This story is the loss of that testimony, and the gaining of something else. It is an homage to the secret and unseen, like the gently flowing, indigo flowers of *Dalea tentaculoides*—an endangered species in the legume family with tentacle-like glands. It is a vision of light in my darkest places. Yet, it is not the darkness that casts a haunted shadow over my life, nor my youth. In wilderness, darkness is rich, bottomless, and unimaginably bewitching. In wild spaces as in life, I need not fear the shadows, only my lack of seeing.

Procession of Trees

By late summer in the Sonoran Desert, rain-bearing winds travel upward from tropics of the Pacific Ocean, following in the footsteps of rising, heated air and shifts in wind flow. Once they arrive, monsoon thunderstorms are rare and dramatic. Muddy, detritus-filled water pounds through parched landscapes, while the arid desert soils take a deep drink. In the cities, streets transform into rivers, and stores can abruptly close their doors. Some residents of the desert poetically recognize the coming of these storms as las aguas—the waters. Yet, primarily during the winter months, the Sonoran Desert experiences soft, quenching storms that are blown in from the west. These more predictable bouts of weather are known as las equipatas—little packages of rain—a name incorporating the Spanish and Yaqui-Mayo languages.

To live in Sonora is to witness the significance of motion and migration. Seasonal weather fronts serve as a reminder that our community is deeply rooted in an ecology of movement. The flora and fauna of the desert tell us this has always been the case, a landscape that looks beyond its borders to remember its history, or to shape a new one: a story older than its caliche crust. As difficult as it may be to imagine, about half of the Sonoran Desert's biota has tropical ancestors borne from a warm but damp climate. When the region became more arid, the plants adapted, evolving to become more tolerant to dry conditions. Their memory is instilled in the biodiversity of this region, with species like the iconic saguaro cactus, evolving hand in hand with the Sonoran Desert, or the organ pipe cactus, which occupied dry tropics nearer to the equator before migrating up to the Sonoran Desert just 3,500 years ago.

In the north third of the Sonoran Desert, an eighteen-foot wall of steel eviscerates this region sculpted by movement, endangering species including jaguars, ocelots, and Mexican gray wolves. Construction along this wall demarking the US-Mexico border has already displaced and destroyed the habitats of countless species great and small. In doing so, the Trump administration flouted key environmental laws, taking advantage of the Illegal Immigration Reform and Immigrant Responsibility Act of 1996, which gives the Department of Homeland Security sweeping authority to defy these regulations. A place defined by its freedom of movement is accompanied by green-eyed politicians seeking to constrain its magic.

—

During periods of flooding, vegetation is at its most vulnerable. Towering trees yield to rising currents, some uprooted from their life-giving soils, and are thrust mercilessly into a temporary but fierce river. When the trees once again meet solid ground, sometimes hundreds of miles from their homeland, they are stripped of everything but their most tenacious characteristics, worn smooth by the traumas of relocation.

When I moved to southern Arizona, I witnessed communities uprooted by deportation. People who provided protective, nourishing habitats from which many took root, vanished. On these occasions, the tenderness of agony is not a sensation one can soon forget. Their homes became lightless, empty corridors from which we could only contemplate the thick brush of nationalism.

If migrants were trees, I imagine them desert ironwoods, towering up to thirty-five feet in height. A nurse tree, the ironwood provides four fundamental ingredients: shade, shelter, soil, and sustenance. These characteristics allow the tree to look after the disadvantaged, perhaps as a cover from the blistering sun, or protection from buffeting winds, or by furnishing a refuge to escape from the snapping jaws of a predator. Ironwoods also infuse the soil with nitrogen, providing a nutrient crucial in plant growth. Even the ironwood's seed pods are gobbled up by wandering animals, supplying a nutritious source of food for many creatures. Upwards of five hundred species of plants and animals are nurtured by ironwoods, including botanical species that are said to grow only beneath its motherly limbs. I can think of many immigrants to Sonora worthy of such a comparison.

I am beneath a sycamore becoming undone.
An abandoned backpack,
a down-turned canister,
a plastic jug that may as well be glass,
as it tears at the part of me that held resolve.

Do words still carry weight?
Do we still yield the capability for change?
I leave without answer.

I am standing on paths that are roots,
spread out, underground
through canyons,
within our cities, seeking
nutrients of justice.

I am beneath a sycamore losing hope
with a child's glove,
a weathered cross,
a vial of painkillers
that could never mend
this broken heart.

I am a man, but sometimes I hate it. It is an inexplicable sensation, dysphoria, defined by Merriam-Webster as "a state of feeling very unhappy, uneasy, or dissatisfied." Sometimes, I am all those things. Sometimes, I am none.

I feel privileged for being so comfortable with my anatomy, for feeling at home with *any* pronoun. I am lucky for that. Still, I lose myself in a suit because it makes me feel like a man, and I am not one. Little acts put me back into my body. During puberty, I took scissors to my face—I never purchased a razor because I was still in facial hair denial—and chopped my bristle until I bled down my parents' sink. I kept cutting at my neck and body, trying to sever the timeline that made me masculine. These scissors stayed in the bottom of a drawer to emerge when I was alone, terrified of this shame being uncovered by my parents. Bodies were eternal, I was taught, and God didn't make mistakes. While gender was not a topic of discussion when I was a kid, the sentiments were unambiguous: men were men, women were women. As leading church authority Dallin H. Oaks put it many years later, "Binary creation is essential to the plan of salvation."

Those like myself, who tilted toward their assigned gender, had choices. I simply chose to be masculine and learned to occupy a fraction of my being. I understood, though, that I could hide from neither God nor myself. We knew what was beneath my clothes, particularly when I succumbed to temptation and shaved my chest bare.

—

Neckties were mandatory on church Sunday; mine was gray with dark diagonal stripes—the sort of discount-clothes-store design that felt appropriate, given that I couldn't have felt more subtracted while wearing it. Entering sacrament meetings was an all-you-can-eat buffet of dysphoria—dressed in a manly-man's costume—while being characterized by every synonym for masculine. It was the churchgoer's way of mingling with the youth, staying involved. Little by little, I gaslit myself into believing they didn't bother me, but in the sanctity of my parents' bathroom, I wept at seeing the precision of their words.

Over the years I failed at finding the person I wanted to be, even in LGBTQ+ spaces where *nonbinary* didn't fit the shape of my spirit. I was looking for revelation and came home with slivers of uncertainty nagging at my subconscious. I concluded I must be faking it, digging too deep. I thought I should ignore this incongruity between mind and body, because when the English language had no word to give meaning to my pains, I felt like I lacked the authority to exist.

For years I had beautiful dreams where I was a different person. I was not male. I was not female. There existed no society to guard the outlines of my gender. I had curly dark hair tinged purple, my body strong and capable. There were mountains carved from clay. I felt myself a part of them. I became as I was born: a person, a spirit, a witness to creation. My God was a tree, an old juniper who had weathered their branches to silver. I knew who I was, not because my language gave me permission, but because I *was*. I existed, and the expansiveness of my being grew with the cultivation of my knowing.

Being born of the earth, between mountains and desert, was a source of great power. I didn't need to define what parts of me were female and which parts were male, fractionalizing my identity until it shattered. I could simply *be* and be kind, love this world because I belonged to it. I was everything as much as I was nothing. My only future was clay as it sifted through my fingers, holding grains of once-deer and once-primrose, and the fragments of fungi that produced the enzymes to decompose their bodies, giving them new form.

Binary creation is not eternal, nor does it exist. Our bodies are biomes for trillions of microbial cells: bacteria, fungi, viruses. The liquid components of our blood, plasma, is 90 percent water, recycled from the tiny bladders of grasshopper mice, from evaporative water that escaped from trees and rivers, and from moisture captured by soil. Perhaps I *am* they, plural, a thing of many things, and a living history of everything that swims through my veins.

Burnice

Shelter. *Refugio*. How often I take it for granted. Today I see the traces of immigrants who walk beside me, their trails of wooden beads and crucifix jewelry tied to the boughs of junipers, guiding them toward canned food, water, and blankets sprawled on cavern floors. I shelter here for different reasons entirely. It is my peaceful place—as foolishly privileged as that may sound—and there's nothing like a chest full of riparian air to clean out the bad spirits of urban life haunting my brain.

Along the trail, most rock is covered with gardens of ferns, golden columbines, and a pallid-tinged succulent with which I shamelessly converse when I'm first to meet the sunrise. Beneath these hanging habitats, in a small watercourse that appears and disappears, canyon tree frogs display their cryptic coloration, a stone-gray mottle that is nearly imperceptible against the underlying volcanic tuff. To the north, these frogs often carry the colors of the Sonoran Desert: beige to green to the salt-and-pepper of granite. They achieve this not by regional genetic adaptation, but by utilizing a special hormone that prompts their color pigment cells to alter the color of their skin.

My boyfriend, Aaron Goldtooth, a math and astrophysics major at the University of Arizona, and Alan Cressler, a naturalist and photographer from Georgia, arise from their slumber and join my saunter through the borderlands. We follow the movement of the stream, walking forward with our arms outstretched, fingers splayed, pushing through vegetation that has all but swallowed the banks of the arroyo. The waterway twists and turns, flowing south into Mexico, to a topography that is filleted open, saguaros standing guard.

Inside the canyon, we continue swatting and tiptoeing, wending our way through the vast and unyielding vegetation that conjures thoughts of dinosaurs and plants overgrown in a distant CO_2-rich past. Nearby, brightly red-chested warblers hop over blankets of dried leaves and cobblestones, eventually diving out of view to their nests cradled in the overgrowth. The warblers, commonly known as painted redstarts—or *Myioborus pictus* if you have an affinity for Latin—have traveled north from Mexico for courtship, males arriving first. They leap along the bank with their red chests puffed, flushing tasty insects from the earth until—several days later—they hear the songs of ashen-gray females. The moment arrives when they couple, joining in duets that flow through the canyon like drafts of fresh air. We stand here, binoculars in hand, making lessons of movement, feeling the distance of traveled wings. This is the United States by definition, by borders that have made physical an arbitrary line. To flora and fauna, this is an island of compatible habitat drawn upward.

Many species are spread between these paths, the imaginary lines and borderlands both political and ecological, not only dissected by a wall of steel but *intersected* by communities of bordering desert and mountain, oak-grassland and chaparral, desert grassland and desert scrub, pine-oak woodland and mixed conifer forest, pine forest and oak woodland. Biomes and borders cover this place like a Venn diagram drawn on a spirograph, providing space for species difficult to imagine from the redrock haunts of the American Southwest. Such is the case with the strange insect *Pselliopus zebra*, so named for its vivid, zebra-like stripes present through its legs, antennae, and wings. It is also a true bug or Hemiptera, an order of insects with specialized mouthparts to feed on plant sap or—more rarely—the blood of animals. Here, one cannot speak of biodiversity without their words being drowned to birdsong.

—

On the Mexican side of the border, about two hundred miles to the southeast, is a colony where my great-grandmother, Burnice Thygerson, was born. Her grandparents fled from the United States to Mexico, arriving in Colonia Dublán in the state of Chihuahua. As early converts to the Mormon faith, they were practitioners of polygamy, with her grandfather taking in five wives.

When the Utah Territory was established in the wake of the Mexican-American War, followers of the church were asked to renounce polygamy or face prosecution. Many families made the difficult decision to travel southward to escape the reach of federal jurisdiction.

By 1910, after many Mormon families settled in northern Mexico, the Mexican Revolution led the country into chaos as bank and crop failures provoked poverty-stricken communities to revolt against their government. Turmoil and instability within Mexico's leadership led to riots and eventually civil war. To avoid conflict, Mormons abandoned their homes and farmlands in Mexico.

Burnice fled across the border with her parents, releasing their livestock to survive on the desert shrubs while they waited out hostilities in El Paso. Within a few months, no longer believing a safe return was possible, they looked onward to Sevier Valley in central Utah.

"During the Revolutionary War," she recalls within her journal,

> the fighting came nearer to our town and Daddy took the family up on some hills, and when it got dark, we could see the flashes of fire from the cannons and [we could] hear loud booms. . . . It wasn't long after this that

we got word that we should all prepare to leave our homes because we were American citizens and to go to El Paso for maybe a couple of weeks. It was a beautiful moonlit summer night. A messenger came to every home saying that we should all leave our homes and be at the railroad station in two hours, which was almost midnight.

—

A century has passed, Burnice is long gone, and I am unstitching my history. I am seven hundred miles from where I was born, yet seven hundred miles closer to the birthplace of Burnice. I am walking in footsteps now long overgrown by skeletonized branches of ocotillo, placing my feet where my family followed a decisive path northward. Today, which my phone claims is November 4, 2019, a drug cartel has murdered nine people from a Mormon colony just over the border. Distant family. Neighbors. Some were spattered with bullets, others burned alive. Three women, six children.

Hardships and privilege. My ancestors emigrated nearly a thousand miles on foot to flee from religious persecution, carrying their possessions in wagons from Illinois to the Great Salt Lake Valley, which was then Mexican territory. In doing so, many of them succumbed to freezing temperatures and illnesses, their bodies abandoned in graves dredged from frozen earth. "Such was the price some pioneers paid," wrote the late prophet Thomas S. Monson. "Their bodies are buried in peace, but their names live on evermore. Tired oxen lumbered, wagon wheels squeaked, brave men toiled, war drums sounded, and coyotes howled. But the faith-inspired and storm-driven pioneers pressed on." Later, many of my grandparents fled to present-day Mexico, only to come back to the United States to escape the reach of instability and warfare.

Mexico is like a second home to me and to many Mormon

descendants. I feel a sense of obligation and empathy for those crossing this border today. I think of Burnice, and my great-grandfather. I think of people coming home and making home. "They take our jobs, our country, they're dangerous," my father would say around our dinner table. "Then so are we," I would retort, teeth gritted, waiting to persuade my family toward empathy for others, which, by extension, included myself. I always believed that the comparison between Mormons and undocumented immigrants was inevitable. Our tragedies were not similar, nor were the stories that unraveled before migrants arrived at this border, but there lies a lesson in parallels and juxtaposition. A wall of steel and disparities of fate: incarceration without due process, child separation, life with cartels, and individuals who served in the US military only to be sent back south. Mormons and their progeny are not only immigrants to this country but emigrants from it. Our realities as citizens of the United States are cut by a thin trail of decisions that have defined our destinies and given shape to the privileges in which we participate. Our feet were burned red under these same soils, traveling in the same direction, for the same sense of safety sought by migrants entering this country today.

This journey, the first to what was then Mexican territory, is remembered by Mormon youth when they take part in Trek: a three-day religious expedition through western wilds. Sometimes donning hand-stitched clothing—bonnets, dresses, or suspenders—they walk over sun-parched expanses ferrying handcarts through river and rock, reflecting on the heavy sacrifices paid by their ancestors. But these privileges were not birthrights. They took purchase in well-wrought soils, soils that cost lives, good health, and worldly comforts.

Little stirs in the moonlit desert, except for the owl. She is female and old for her species, though nothing of her appearance speaks to this. Her wisdom felt rather than seen.

She looks down at us with sunny irises, her head cocked, feathers tasseling as she shuffles on the branches of a lone cottonwood. She is the color of rust, white waves traced down her chest, with black bars over her eyes like angry eyebrows. Her wings unfold, her body inches forward, she wobbles as she adjusts her weight. Then she dives, sweeping over the windshield, her wings T-posed, pupils contracted.

My father pays no attention to her gray beauty, whispering under his breath while practicing a speech, his hands motioning in the air to emphasize inaudible words. His intonations mirror church sacrament meetings, each sentence ending with a drop in tone, evoking kindness behind a fierce, patriarchal authority. He pauses to clutch both hands around the steering wheel, swerving back and forth as we rattle into the valley to the howl of Fleetwood Mac.

In our headlights, a featureless expanse, eroded into red clay and pale gravel. Save for a few rocks weathered into ghoulish shapes, there is nothing. No plants. No cliffs. Just the earth and air; terrain less intimate desert lovers might call impoverished. What I saw was something vast and untamable, a beauty that knew adversity and instantly took its shape. After driving for nearly an hour, we park and look upward, watching the blood moon drift into the cumulus.

—

My father learned he could use the desert as a religious prop, using my safe spaces to extend the long arms of the church. It was a way to reach me. He knew this. I was stuck with him, he with me. We were locked in a tug-of-war, fighting for ground, for personhood, for faith. He ripped at the threads that held my heart together. But this. This was an unpardonable betrayal. He claimed he only intended the best for me, but it mattered little when his callused hands wrung this soul of everything but its bitterness.

"We all have choices," he spoke above the silence, "and those choices have consequences."

Today he teaches of the Second Coming, when Jesus is said to come down and cast his judgement. In Mormon doctrine, there are degrees of glory that are assigned to you once Christ returns. These three kingdoms are the Celestial, Terrestrial, and Telestial. If you have committed any of the most heinous sins, you are not assigned a kingdom. Instead, you are sent into outer darkness to roam with Satan, where you will encounter "weeping and [the] gnashing of teeth," a description vague enough to be a Rorschach test for our deepest fears. Each of these kingdoms is compared to our night sky, with God as our sun—our universal center place. In the Celestial Kingdom, like the sun, we are given the full presence of God. The Terrestrial Kingdom, like the moon, has some of God's presence and light. But the Telestial Kingdom, like the stars, has no presence of God. Related to this is the process of sealing, which eternally sustains your earthly family relationships in the afterlife. Families who are not sealed together are believed to be forever separated after death or after the Second Coming, whichever comes first. Until 2019, homosexual members could be excommunicated for their sexual orientation, voiding such sealings.

"Jonathan," my father continued, "the blood moon is a signal that the end-times are near." He paused, looking over to see my distraught expression. "You will be there at the Second Coming. You must make faithful choices or be taken from God and your family." His words held still.

While we had these conversations, I was coming to terms with my sexuality, terrified of this so-called sin that walked with me, so inseparable from my self that it felt like my shadow. I knew the day would come when I would be punished for my queerness, when I would lose my family—and God—forever, and it was my fault. I felt that deeply. I felt responsible for the separation of my family. I felt responsible for my sexuality. When our prophet Gordon B. Hinckley passed away, I felt responsible for his death. I thought it to be punishment for my feelings, my inclinations, as if each member carried with them a piece of the church, and when they found that irreconcilable part of themselves that strained their belief, there was real, physical harm done to the faith. So I spent my time carving gaps of understanding between me and everyone else, knowing I was bound to collapse toward this so-called wretchedness, toward a place of eternal darkness. Whatever lay beneath, I wanted to go it alone, to protect others from falling with me. Then the prophesy fulfilled itself. There was weeping, there was gnashing of teeth, and I went to a dark and uncertain place. But this prophesy was realized by my family, my community, myself.

In our ward, I was never taught where gay people were sent, but I feared the worst, assuming an eternity in outer darkness. This was reiterated by apostle Dallin H. Oaks when he described homosexuality from the lens of scripture: "Do not choose eternal death, according to the will of the flesh and the evil which is therein, which giveth the spirit of the devil power to captivate, to bring you down to hell, that he may reign over you in his own kingdom."

When I was a young boy, these fears manifested in dreams of an apocalypse. Angels clambered down, cold and gray like statues, through charcoal-black cloud cover. Their long claws curled downward, eyes bulging, flesh decomposed. Disembodied voices whispered as the angels approached my bedroom, prowling through our city for the unfaithful like well-trained canines. They ripped open my door and crawled above me, wings scraping walls like stone blades. With a fist raised toward the sky, they stated my living was a betrayal to the church. I knew then, even when I lacked the words to say it, that I was born unworthy.

Eight years old, I am in a font;
a baptism, to welcome
the sensation of drowning.
Stripped naked, dressed in white,
in a room while someone watches.
They cleanse me of myself and tag me
with a number, to be pure. Worthy of
my body. A sacred rite that feels
like a violation.

Song Dog

Coyotl.

Barking dog.

Your name is a memory of Nahuatl language, the same spoken by Aztecs and Toltecs of Mexico. You do not bark, but sing, wistfully, from frostbitten canyons in the early morning.

I hear the sorrow in your voice. I know your grizzled fur. Your golden eyes, the color of tree sap, often glisten with grief.

You are no trickster, nor thief. You are vulnerable and misunderstood, like me. You are a disciple of aloneness. For that, people are wary. But it is not you they truly fear, it is themselves, as they have given you their worst characteristics.

When I was younger, I knew you only from your parched flesh. After collecting a bounty for your scalp, my neighbors draped what was left of your body over their fence. "Let them see it," they said to me, believing your limp form would frighten your young pups away from the farm. I picked you up anyway, cradling your lifeless body between my arms, running my fingers through your coarse gray fur. I placed you gently in a patch of sunflowers, assuming you liked them as much as I did. If you knew no kindness in life, I thought, perhaps you could sense it in death.

I am with you regardless of your perception. You were, after all, always there for me. I saw you lurking protectively behind the piñons where I sat curled, distraught by my own uncertainties.

You also accompanied Aaron and me through our first back-packing trip together down the Dirty Devil River. You sang us to sleep behind a deep, tunneling canyon smoked in blue light. I almost broke free of the tent and searched for you, intoxicated by your cacophonous laughter, like a siren's song. I knew no harm would await me, though. You are all charm and no bite. Even when I moved to southern Arizona, you were among the first to welcome me to this new home, walking just a few feet away, twisting your head inquisitively.

You are known by many names and pronunciations: Iisaw, Ma'ii, Ban, Kahy-oh-tee, Kahy-oht. Yet, all I need is your voice, and I will know you are there, roaming behind the desert's empty mirage.

When my parents weren't watching, I
played with fox. We chased
each other through cattails,
against the deep water,
where damselflies dashed
through our vision
like eye spots.

When you chased me, I let you close,
so close I could bury my face
into your mud-red fur
and breathe you into me.

Sometimes, I turned back,
to memorize your brown eyes and
white tummy and black feet
that looked like toe socks.

My sister was less receptive
of fox. Running, screaming.
Rabies! Rabies!
Fox learned
that reciprocation
is trust.

You found a mate.
You moved on.
I moved on.
But I treasure you,
my old friend,
and hope you feel
as wanted,
as loved,
as I felt
with you.

An Evening with Tyto alba

An owl clutches a branch above me, her face round and compressed like a crafted opal disc. She is perched on the barren, wintered limbs of an old cottonwood, revealing little more than her outline—a broken mosaic of silver and brown feathers, her two black eyes like coals set deep in snowpack. She calls, the canyon falls silent, and I zip my coat, expecting a long and cold night ahead.

I continue up canyon, thinking of omens and owls. "Bad juju," some of my friends would say. I never believed their malice. Quite the contrary. I believed owls were victims to false equivalence, creatures that, by chance or circumstance, occupied spaces that give normal people the heebie-jeebies: cemeteries, depopulated buildings, places where absence is filled with a childlike fear of the imagined. But I found safety and peace in nocturnal haunts. I adored owls and unjustifiably concluded the feeling was mutual.

The owl settled there, frozen, beneath two emerald shields painted on the canyon wall. Her face soon came into view, outlined by a heart of feathers, and there she posed, in full Audubon glory: *Tyto alba*. A barn owl. I looked closely and found the softness in her, but the words ran on repeat through my head:

Witch, witch, witch.

A hood of feathers covered her skull and cloaked her body: a blue-gray mottle with white arrow patches tipped black. Her eyes were so dark, unimaginably dark, balanced above a needle-thin beak, curved and sharp like surgical scissors. Fine-tuned to hunt, she moved silently with serrated wings and bared a concave face to focus sound—ears positioned asymmetrically to determine the height of her prey. I continued past her, approaching the painted shields to find an ancient hand pecked into the sandstone, a thousand years old, its fingers several sizes too long. I looked above me and she stood still, a hovering white ghost.

Witch, witch, witch.

If my paternal grandmother were alive, she would tell me those words. Her terror of owls, the omens and witchcraft. She would beg for a rifle to exterminate "that thing" from her sterile and paranoid world, and I would deny her the opportunity. Her view was one of isolation—her religion, her species, her race. She sharpened her slurs with hard *R*'s and stereotypically queer gestures. What a lonely world in which to live.

When my grandmother passed, I was just beginning to understand my sexuality. Had she learned, given regard to the desert just beyond her door, she would find an inclusive habitat, home to many animals who participate in same-sex hanky-panky: ravens, foxes, lizards, snakes, spiders, bears (*actual* bears, but also the kind endemic to Katy Perry concerts), dragonflies, and yes, barn owls. She would find asexual, or apogamous, ferns, birds that project an opposite-sex appearance, and so many creatures in so many colors, sizes, and shapes. They are teachers, seers, revelators of body and spirit.

—

In the church, I was taught about badness. Alcohol, sex, coffee, temptation. For my grandmother, owls were just another tick on the list. As I got older, the shame developed with me: I am bad for being human. I am bad for drinking wine with friends. I am bad for the coffee above my stove. I am bad for wanting to be loved, to be touched. I am bad for being human. I am bad. Beyond doctrine, beyond belief, the ways I was taught to engage with my body were perpetual. Soon, wild creatures became euphemisms for these "animalistic" desires—unpredictable, ungovernable, irrepressible. Control the wild, church elders implied, and restrain yourself. Be obedient. Live to die, die to live.

I yearn for someone to open this cage, set me free from myself, but it is hard when the lock is forged from flesh. *I am bad* because I was a child who had the arrogance to be himself.

—

I am in bed, hearing the muffled song of an owl in the Chinese elm she always wanted to fell. I look out to my grandmother's house next door, her bathroom light illuminated against monsoon clouds gathered in response to the warm, moist air off the Gulf of Mexico. Unbeknownst to me, she is dead. I slide my hands on the lock of my window, propping it open to listen to the owl speak. Its voice cuts through the air like talons, a new testament divined from three short calls in the wake of August.

They Take Our Bodies

Our body is a temple, or so we are told, because it is contained by the Mormon church. There comes a time in every Mormon's life when we are asked to give a little bit of our bodies. This trespass is slow; it needs to be slow to work. Little by little, we give our individuality in exchange for our loyalty, our leadership for submission, and our humanity for guilt. Our bodies become property in the eyes of men, churchly men. It is the most subtle and perverse demand.

For my sister, this request came when she was a young child. She was molested in a room down the street from our house. She came home and told my parents, who did nothing. Because it was hard. Because she was "too young to remember" but wasn't. Because they were taught from an early age to be submissive to patriarchy, to men who take power.

Women are asked to contain and remove their bodies from desire, to cover their shoulders, to be modest, to control the thoughts of men. We are all taught to be virgins at any expense, that rape renders a person worthless. All members are asked not to engage with their own bodies, to never touch themselves in private, or touch another consenting partner. When you do touch yourself, even by accident, or have sex because you are human and falter on their unreachable demands, they use it to justify taking more of yourself. Worse, you beg them to do it. Because you feel guilty, dirty. Then, as we grow older, they take our underwear, an act so intimate and invasive, and replace them with homogenous garments to strip us of something deeper than clothes. Uncomfortable, unflattering, out-of-time. These are the intentions of garments meant to be ugly and undesirable and to make us feel that way by wearing them.

Perhaps that is the ultimate request from this godforsaken church, to give them control of our bodies until we cannot give more, and then—when we need our bodies back because we are a woman, gay, trans, or simply human—they convince us to take our own lives. It hardly feels like these suicides are suicides anymore. Not when the church knows they are responsible, not when they know it's happening, not when people beg for compassion and get a heart full of guilt.

"You make think you are happy, but you are not"

These were the words mailed to my house from the church when I resigned. Even after leaving the church, my body was leveraged as collateral. I felt responsible for how church members perceived me, because I was now the only way anyone I loved was getting out. I didn't want to be a stereotype, I didn't want to be *that* ex-Mormon, but this was how the church kept me in a chokehold, how it maintained control of my body. I couldn't drink, because they would see me, and think poorly of me because of it. I couldn't pierce my ears or buy coffee. I couldn't get tattoos. I couldn't talk about my sexuality or hold hands with my partner. I couldn't curse. I couldn't cope with my depression or speak openly about the pain of losing my religion and community. All of this because of ten words dropped in the mailbox: *You may think you are happy, but you are not.* Every time I proved them wrong, I stepped further into the faith, and further away from the person I wanted to be.

What I want? Fuck. I don't even know anymore.

Life is ephemeral, like desert water.
Regret not its stillness.
Idle is a deep well.
Faith, a deep well.
For all bow their heads
to your creation.

Above us there is a sign that reads:

> *Smuggling and illegal immigration may be*
> *encountered in this area.*
> *Do not travel alone.*
> *Avoid encounters with suspicious groups.*
> *Avoid traveling at night.*
> *Dial 911 to report illegal activity.*

This is how I imagine Sonora: sereness paired with pastels, bones with brittlebush, and death with movement. There is a Georgia O'Keeffe painting of a similar place titled *From the Faraway, Nearby*, where longing is felt in feathery shades of pink and blue. A deer skull centers the composition. Sinuous, branch-like antlers are twisted behind it. Further back, there are only pastels, a sunset faded to infinity, badlands absorbing color like an arid sponge. Here, there is another color: green, used feverishly in mesquite and saguaros, in jangly-armed chollas, and in plumes of ocotillo stalks spilled outward like tail feathers. Here, horizon lines take shape by Madrean Sky Islands that blur the boundary between the temperate and tropical, so distant as to fade into blue bands a shade from invisibility. There are fifty-seven mountains comprising these veritable islands, known for their biological diversity as well as their rarity. They are, as naturalist Robert Villa once described them to me, the "tide pools" of the Sonoran

Desert, refugees of its past and present biota. Seven thousand unique and ecologically important species inhabit these refuges, including coatis, ocelots, and jaguars. The faraway is nearby indeed.

Alan Cressler clutches the steering wheel next to me. Since I moved to Tucson, he has flown in from Georgia every year, joining me to spend weeks around the US-Mexico border, splitting our time between the Sonoran Desert and the Madrean Sky Islands. Today we drift between these ecological boundaries, desert and island, following rough muddy roads as far as we dare to drive before proceeding on foot, looking for rare ferns discernible only to Alan's keen eyesight. The path takes us heel over hand through fissures of black rock and knee-deep seeps of spring water. An agave plant greets us by shooting its long, needle-tipped spines deep into our thighs. Hours pass, coatis scamper through—tails raised like question marks—then we are dumped back in the desert, glimpsing border patrol checkpoints through walls of creosote. A white sign reads: *Stop Here for Immigration Inspection*. Just before it, an unintentionally apt warning to *Watch for Ice on Roadway*, presumably for the kind less abundant in the heat of southern Arizona.

In a few miles, we pass through an area we called the PLBI—short for the Parallel Line Bubba Intaglios. We named it after its grisly destruction: parallel scars, row after row, etched from the earth and lacking even the smallest trace of life—no plants, no lichens, no algae, no fungi, and certainly no ferns. No friendly faces from which I could recognize heads from tails. Graveyards, I also call them.

Over the last several years, these "glyphs" were carved by border patrol vehicles, churning through soil and vegetation to search for migrants. They drive through formerly roadless regions to herd people out of the overgrowth and into captivity, sometimes accompanied by a circus of helicopters and motorbikes. In the aftermath is an interwoven network of two-track

trenches—totaling thousands of miles along the border wall—
that can be seen from the far reaches of space. Some of these
tracks extend into wilderness areas that are required by law to
remain roadless. Scars on scars on scars.

Once immigrants are captured after walking hundreds of
miles, they are hauled away. Severely dehydrated, ill from infec-
tion and malnutrition, they may tempt fate by devouring cacti.
Stomach ailments usually follow, throats swell shut, and dehy-
dration weakens them to the brittle end. In these tragic circumstances, choices are made between life and liberty. Many have no
choice at all, journeying both to the United States and through
this realm of being.

Beginning with the Clinton administration, border patrol
began employing an inhumane "prevention through deterrence"
program, which increased the presence of agents in border cities
like Nogales, a few hours south of Tucson. Their intention was to
push migrants into inhospitable areas like the Sonoran Desert,
where resources like food and water are scarce and the odds of
surviving the journey are low. Over time, and after many need-
less deaths, they thought it would deter undocumented immigrants from entering the United States. Historian Rachel Nolan
has defined it as "a legal euphemism for leaving people to die on
purpose."

Today, one person dies on the US-Mexico border every day
on average, and this statistic has held true for over two decades.
Their bodies lace the desert in mummified poses. Thousands
are located and taken to the medical examiner, but others are
disassembled, carried by wind, water, and the jaws of curious
scavengers, remembered by articles of clothing and fragments of
bleached white bones.

Alan wandered ahead, deciding to curve around the canyon while I walked its upper ledge searching for ferns. It wasn't
long before I saw the camouflage hat, tucked in the overgrowth,

downtrodden and stained with mud. Just beyond was a ball of white, partially submerged in the clay.

Bone?

No, *shell.*

From the Pacific Ocean.

In the Sonoran Desert.

Glycymeris, a bittersweet clam, its shape sprawled outward like a porcelain bowl. Its back polished flat, marked by a drill hole that never punched through. It was old, Hohokam, a shell bead-pendant, which was broken and refashioned into a ring-bead for earrings or a necklace. About eight hundred years ago, it was carried from the Gulf of California, held in the sack of a traveler, crossing over a hundred miles, defying borders physical and imagined.

—

As denizens of the Southwest, we are asked to reconsider borders. When I was a child, my parents took me on my first trip to the Bears Ears, returning to Grayson, which would become present-day Blanding. My ancestors arrived here in the early 1900s. Many of them, like Burnice, had fled from Mexico, often moving between central and southeastern Utah after their return to the US.

We visited the Edge of the Cedars State Park Museum, constructed near a small village occupied from AD 825 to 1225. Near the back room was a sash, illuminated in dim light. Composed of red feathers, save for a bluish patch near its center, the sash was joined together with the pelt of a tassel-eared squirrel, and attached with ropes derived from yucca. The feathers were iridescent, plucked from scarlet macaws nine hundred years ago, and cradled into an alcove in southeastern Utah. It remained there until 1955. After studying the object, researchers concluded it was made with local materials, suggesting the feathers were not traded. Rather, macaws were brought (and, current evidence suggests, also bred) in the deserts of the Colorado Plateau. Northbound travelers also carried with them pockets full of copper bells, cacao, marine shells, and *Zea mays*, otherwise known as maize or corn, a crop derived from a Mesoamerican species of grass known as teosinte that preceded these exchanges. In the years after examining the sash, I witnessed carvings of scarlet macaws near the Bears Ears formation, their curved beaks barely agape, skirting over the stone pallet to static-posed humans, arms outstretched as if to express the broad reach of their people.

—

Prior to the Treaty of Guadalupe Hidalgo of 1848 following the Mexican-American War, the American Southwest was Mexican territory. Before that, when travelers were carrying macaws and marine shells nearly a thousand years ago, they were moving through a borderless expanse between the Bears Ears—and the American Southwest in toto—to the Gulf of California. A border cracked ancestral land like a fragment of mica, defining who was Indigenous and who was illegal.

When migrants arrive in the United States seeking asylum, they may be returning to their ancestral homes, traveling paths carved deeply by stories. When migrants pass from this world, they do so in the presence of old spirits, returning to clay in footprints of the past.

—

Solitude is a word of contradictions. I knew this when I was ten years old. We traveled to the San Rafael Swell on the night of the winter solstice, my oldest brother's birthday. With Navajo Sandstone illuminated in silver blades of moonlight, we found the man's body. He traveled from Michigan to the San Rafael

Reef, stripped his boots, and crawled into the back seat of his car. With the static crackling of bats zipping overhead, he took a hose from the exhaust through the window and ended his life. We found his body facedown between the seats. His arm was outstretched toward the door as if to question his decision. The car was still running.

I found his boot prints that evening, walking the river's edge as if to leave this world in beauty. In a moment of reflection, I witnessed his last moment, how his eyes must have glimmered with stars that stretched over the Muddy Creek. Nearby, crickets sang in chorus from mounds of ricegrass and vermillion Chinle mudstone. Then they stopped mid-song, surrendered to a meditation of earth, wind, and water. I thought I felt his presence in this river, its shade—an olive green—stripped of lucid color in twilight. I thought I could deconstruct his decision, find the trail of longing that carried him across a country to end his life. Could peace and disorder coexist? What was revealed to him as seconds slipped toward nonexistence? I dipped my fingers through the leaden current, wanting its cold sting to impart something of hardship, of conciliation between mind and body, of decisions that didn't make sense in my child eyes.

—

I remembered this when I was a teenager and determined to make a choice, running my fingers down the cold steel of a blade, wanting to end it once and for all. There were moments when I would have given anything to talk to someone, but doing so would reveal my sexuality. So, I stayed silent. Dangerously silent. I missed too much school and, eventually, I was taken to juvenile court, pleading for mental health care that they and my parents seemed so reluctant to secure. The judge, a man known for his homespun style of justice who tried to separate a child from their lesbian parents, ordered me to visit a psychologist, but it came with a poison pill: if I exhibited signs of mental illness, *any* signs, he would send me to a residential treatment center up north.

I don't remember where he wanted to send me exactly, but I do remember being scared. I remember numbness. Panic attacks. At its worst, my arms moved uncontrollably over my chest. I threw up every night, unable to sleep, troubled by chest pain and palpitations. I heard rumors of facilities where children were veritable prisoners, sent to solitary confinement, physically, mentally, sexually abused by workers or peers, surrounded by people who were dangerously unhinged. Those who came back were changed, I was told, and not for the better.

When I visited the psychologist—accompanied by my parents because the law dictated such for minors—I lied.

"Everything is fine," I said. "It was just a misunderstanding." What I couldn't share was my depression, my anxiety, my nightmares that never went away—dreams where I am running but can't find help, crying in sobs scarcely fit for my body, calling home in a cold sweat. Sometimes I looked forward to sleeping, knowing the demons I might encounter, because at least I could escape my nightmares. The between sleep was a sacred space where I learned what was beyond my eyes and mind. In another reality, I hope this was when I came out of the closet and got help for my problems. I bet that version of me is happier. The issue I encountered with Utah's judicial and education systems is that both offered veiled threats over legitimate support, much in the same way that manically burning down the forest doesn't help wolf populations. You may see more of them in a frenzy for their lives, but you can be cocksure it isn't a sign of them rebounding.

And then I was sent back to school.

I was beaten shortly thereafter. A group of students caught me in a chokehold in front of the library, slamming me into a locker door before bringing me to the ground, arms snapped behind my back. Heavy-duty metal staplers were thrown at my head as slurs dropped from their lips like hot coals. Now, years later, I remember powerful words that diminished my experiences as an LGBTQ+ youth, words like *bullying* that reduced assault, rape, and homicide—the realities of queer children—to playground banter. I was told that it would get better by television personalities whose experiences were only scarcely similar to my own, as if anguish was a rite of passage to be forgotten and overcome. What I needed most was validation. No one told me that the actions taken against me were *wrong*. No one told me these transgressions were real and serious, that my mental struggles were justified. There were times when "it gets better" and "depression is a chemical imbalance" felt as if I alone was responsible.

Solitude. I always found solitude. One definition of the word unravels to heartache, the other: salient power. On the brink of ending my life, I chose the latter. I chose to be deeply, madly in love with aloneness. When stripped of everything, I walked this path deep into the desert, revealing the double helix of a word spanning peace and torment. Georgia O'Keeffe evoked the duality of solitude as she painted the skeletons of great creatures. "The skulls were there and I could say something with them," she writes. "To me they are as beautiful as anything I know. To me they are strangely more living than the animals walking around—hair, eyes and all, with the tails switching. The bones seem to cut sharply to the center of something that is keenly alive on the desert even though it is vast and empty and untouchable—and knows no kindness with all its beauty."

Boys can't be with boys
on Prom Night. On any
night. I go into the desert
alone, broken. An
auditorium of stars
domes into dawn.
Wisps of smoke curl
around my chest, beckoning
the final track of moonlight.

The Letters I Never Wrote

How can I be honest with grief when those close to me are complicit in the suffering?

I am protecting someone who told me that gay people should be executed in concentration camps, and I said nothing. They dragged me by the neck to a vehicle, beat me inside the cab, as they sensed my growing disbelief.

I am protecting someone by forgetting to mention that a woman stripped her clothes when I was six years old. She took me to an unfamiliar room and asked me if I wanted to see more, which I did not. She asked me if I wanted to place my hands on her body, which I did not.

People said they were ashamed to be seen with me. They told me my family was better off without me. When they noticed my neurological differences, they mocked my incapability. Through it all, I was blamed for their actions, and I did nothing.

I struggle to write with sincerity knowing there is so much more I cannot say, as other people would know I spoke of individuals within my church and community. I do not seek revenge. All I want is my voice, and I write because that now feels like wringing water from shriveled branches.

When I left the church, I regained my truth and integrity, but I was asked by them to keep silent. To be anything other than happy, to have scars that run deeper than doctrine, was affirmation, to them, of divine punishment for resignation. I have covered my tracks that lead to grief, knowing they seek to weaponize it. I have tried for so long to keep my spirit out of reach from them, and therefore, myself, but I have grown tired of wearing a mask I thought to have already removed. I was not given a choice between happiness and truth, but if that were the ultimatum I was given, I would choose truth. Always truth.

I am protecting no one and everyone, just as this is not written about any one person, but many. At its end, childhood is disassembled like a fresh kill. Assault is followed by opportunity, like scavengers riding thermals in circular motions, their powerful wings outstretched, preparing to indulge in life that has already been taken.

Who am I really protecting? I know it is not myself.

West of the Santa Cruz River life and death join in a raucous celebration. Performers dance through the streets in bell-lined dresses, ringing to reanimate the spirits of the deceased. The dancers' faces are concealed by painted skulls, some traced with lilac-colored flowers, others with lace-like spiderwebs.

Día de Muertos, Day of the Dead, is a holiday celebrated throughout Mexico in late October and early November, likely originating from an Aztec festival honoring Mictēcacihuātl, the goddess of the underworld and afterlife. The celebration invites those who have died to rejoin the living, if only for a day, and if only in spirit. It is an opportunity to remember and reflect on family. In Tucson, this and other traditions flow together as the All Souls Procession, an event attracting over a hundred thousand attendees crammed together into a single street, moving southward in unison, a sea of bobbing skulls. The celebration brings the inward out, in grief and in death.

A preacher in a trench coat screams that we are all going to hell—the gays, the frolickers, the Mexicans. I hope he's right. I'd love to stay in touch. I joined these celebrations to taste the richness of mortality, as bitter as it is sweet, like cacao that stings the tongue. Signs are raised above the crowd to honor the dead, each plastered with photographs of loved ones and items of special significance: jewelry, plush animals, tattered shoes found near the US-Mexico border. Joining the procession is a giant urn, attended by four individuals dressed in red cloaks. Messages to the dead are dropped inside the receptacle and taken to a stage at the end of the line. When the walking stops, the urn is engulfed in flames. Grief is spoken through a thin thread of smoke.

—

Smoke now rises from chimneys as families gather around altars of the deceased in their private homes. Faces of grandparents and small children flicker orange in the candlelight. During the pandemic, Día de Muertos celebrations are canceled but ever needed. By summer of 2020, COVID-19 has already claimed thousands of lives in Tucson and the numbers keep rising. Arizona has the highest cases per capita in the world, over twenty thousand of which are residents of the Tucson area.

Aaron and I have been taking late night walks around Tucson to witness a vibrant city turned dormant. Coerced into isolation for nearly a year, a consequence of COVID-induced transportation and work roadblocks, I began searching for tiny ecosystems—pockets in Tucson where the city yielded to the inundation of the desert. Sometimes the wild manifested as an individual plant that pushed back against the tarmac, but these spaces provided fresh air outside an otherwise claustrophobic apartment, where we had but five hundred square feet to plot wildly urban escapes.

One of my favorite discoveries was desert milkweed—a plant with long, slender stems and pale yellow flowers. Its petals are almost always slicked back, trailing the unfortunately (or aptly?) named corona, the flashy upper section of the flower. Desert milkweed is indigenous to the Sonoran Desert and adaptable to city conditions, often finding inhabitable spaces on street corners or against the walls of buildings. However, desert milkweed is the nexus of a much broader ecosystem. As an attractive source of pollen and sustenance, it supplies a wide population of insects with the ingredients to persist. Earlier in the season, the plant was covered in monarchs, milkweeds being the chosen food for their caterpillar youngins. As adults, they come back to relish in the flowers, faces full of pollen, wings outstretched like delicate panels of honey-stained glass.

When I was lucky, I encountered wasps, like those in the genus *Prionyx*, or thread-waisted wasps, so named due to their thin, toothpick-sized waists and sometimes vibrantly orange abdomens. However, I grew a motherly love for *Pepsis*, or tarantula hawks. With curlicue, blue-black antennae and a temperament few could appreciate, these parasitoid wasps prowl for tarantulas in the overgrowth of Sonora. When the female hawk finds a den, she pierces the spider with her quarter-inch stinger, paralyzing it. She proceeds to lay her eggs in its still-alive body. Once the little ones hatch, the larvae feast on the tarantula's yummy inner flesh, providing them with an ample source of nutrients. The newborns are careful to keep the spider alive as long as their voracious appetites can handle. Vital organs are off the menu. With full bellies, grown tarantula hawks emerge from their burrow to feed on milkweed flowers and complete their life cycle, fulfilling their destinies that stitch life and death together.

The year weathered onward, the plants vanished to a snap of colder weather. When our garden habitat went dormant, Aaron and I traveled further northward, climbing to the top of a car garage above the streets of Tucson. From up there, I had high hopes of glimpsing comets, or distant planets, or migratory birds through the haze of city pollution. But I saw nothing, and found that equally fulfilling. Back home, maskless parties rumbled our floorboards and alleys filled with piles of their garbage. Sick people gathered behind our paper-thin walls and encouraged my descent into living like a raccoon: emerging discreetly under the cover of darkness, eyes peeled around every corner, hissing at pedestrians, skittering to the mailbox and back with my paws pinched around my prize of electricity bills.

For the first time during the pandemic, nearly five months since the stay-at-home orders began, I felt truly isolated. Friends were sick, exposed, or dying. The oldest among them called with last wishes, for reassurances that I would carry their life's work forward. Then there were the counter-experiences that came from students, leadership, from a community who once promised health and safety to be their top priority but made decisions that exposed their greed and apathy. I knew, then, that my confidence in humanity would never completely heal, that "if it financially benefits us" would forever underline any well-intentioned statements.

But Aaron and I came back to this garage to take in the wonderful nothing. In each of us, a little bit of humanity to mend hearts and spirits. This was our opportunity, a procession of sorts, to find a piece of kinship and, further south, to find wildness in plants adapting to *their* scary new world. Together, they held us whole. Hope, like Día de Muertos celebrations, became a matter of repackaging our grief. "Remember," I said, looking over to see his face dimly illuminated, "six years ago, we met for the first time. Then you stayed. Weeks turned to months. Months turned to years. The first time we met was also the last time we were ever truly apart. I am more fortunate for having you with me. Now, more than ever."

June 26, 2015

Dear Aaron,

I miss you already. How is your visit with our friend in Salt Lake City?

My colleague and I have settled in DC after much commotion. We missed our first flight, the second was canceled when the engine exploded. Believe it or not, the passengers weren't terribly keen on joining Amelia Earhart or plummeting nose-first into the Mississippi, although the pilot was gung-ho to continue at low altitude. The third flight went smoothly, although a storm was brooding in Washington, and we circled over soybean fields in Ohio for the remainder of the hour.

I think I am most taken by the Atlantic's humidity. It makes a desert creature such as myself feel breathless. Who knew air could be so heavy, paper so flaccid, and hair so curled and knotted? Otherwise, it is beautiful here. We took a walk through a sculpture garden at the National Gallery of Art under a piercing lapis sky. I became enamored by this particular bronze rabbit. He looked rather like a cryptid or something from H. G. Wells' *The Island of Dr. Moreau.* His paw was raised ever so thoughtfully against his chin to play upon Rodin's *The Thinker.* It warms my heart to see my little lagomorphic companion duly honored for his intellect. On that note, I assume you would object to my bringing him home? I think a behemothic jackrabbit could make quite the statement.

I know you were excited to hear I visited the National Gallery of Art. Through all the Rembrandts, Picassos, and two exquisite portraits from Van Gogh himself, it was *Ginevra de' Benci* that truly struck me—the 15th-century aristocrat with a sulky gaze amid russet Italian fields. Just below her lip, a nearly invisible blemish bears Leonardo da Vinci's fingerprint, preserved in carbon black for the last five hundred years. As a painter who long admired his work from dusty books in rural libraries, seeing this microscopic touch of humanity nearly brought tears to my eyes. His painting is the closest thing in this museum to a revelation. It is as if he speaks some cryptic truth with every hair-thin stroke. Behind that silvered, dragging beard is a man who peers through a spyhole between vision and intellect and yearns to reveal a world behind our impressions. You can look in Ginevra's eyes and feel that encoded in this arrangement of pigment is the secret to light, or wild divinity, or something far too classified to grace our lips. Is this, I wonder, what also compels your love for math and physics?

Apropos to your suggestions, we have visited the National Mall. I feel guilty to report that it made me feel quite conflicted. On one hand, I cherish the principles for which they stand—freedom, democracy, liberty—but I would rather meditate on these concepts in their quarries, wherever those 80,000 tons were stripped for this unsettling achromatic obelisk. I believe public lands are monuments to our restraint. Humble liberties, its truths self-evident, that all are created equal, that they are endowed with certain unalienable Rights. Rights defended, not created, by the government. Rights endowed by our birth planet. My colleague thinks I should visit later, when this entrenched war on public lands is finally over. Maybe then I will see our National Mall with a fresh pair of rose-tinted glasses, not fractured from knocking my head against congressional desks.

On a somewhat related note: I wanted to ask if you checked the news today. The Supreme Court has ruled in *Obergefell v.*

Hodges, acknowledging that marriage is "inherent in the liberty of the person." We can get married! I am looking toward the Supreme Court now, red-eyed, blinking heavily. Since I arrived in DC, I keep seeing this albino squirrel in Henry Park, chirping happily among her stone-colored pals. Perhaps there is some hope for all us oddities, after all. Truth be told, I never thought I would see this day, let alone be *here* when it happened. I only wish you were with me, watching our history open wide in front of us. Right now a crowd has gathered and they are singing and crying, raising their flags skyward. I feel their songs are loud enough for the both of us.

As for me, I am reading Justice Kennedy's majority opinion and I'm trying—ineffectively, it seems—to keep myself together:

> Until the mid-20th century, same-sex intimacy long had been condemned as immoral by the state itself in most Western nations, a belief often embodied in the criminal law. For this reason, among others, many persons did not deem homosexuals to have dignity in their own distinct identity. A truthful declaration by same-sex couples of what was in their hearts had to remain unspoken. . . . Marriage responds to the universal fear that a lonely person might call out only to find no one there. It offers the hope of companionship and understanding and assurance that while both still live there will be someone to care for the other. . . . No union is more profound than marriage, for it embodies the highest ideals of love, fidelity, devotion, sacrifice, and family. In forming a marital union, two people become something greater than once they were.

With nothing more to say, my beloved, I have a flight to catch. I will be with you soon and we can celebrate together, greater than we once were. I regret being so far away.

With all my love,
Jonathan

PS: I wanted to buy you a souvenir, but nothing fit the bill. Every shop sells the strangest presidential curios you've ever seen: Obama bobbleheads (which they did not call Obamabobbles—missed opportunity); presidentures for the elderly folk (OK. I may have made that one up); something called "Chia Obama" that sends sprouts through his scalp like some vegetative Medusa. I tried a farmer's market for local fare and a woman tried earnestly to fill my bag with garlic and onions. But I did find this: a plush barn owl. Now, I know owls are all about bad omens and death in your culture, but he has these little golden eyes and a wing that's slightly upraised as if he's always waving. I couldn't leave him orphaned. He's adorable, like you. Maybe he can be our lesson in breaking stereotypes. I know you will cherish him regardless.

January 24, 2021

Dear Aaron,

    It's funny that I am writing to you, even though you are sitting next to me, asleep, because we are both tired. It has been 319 days since the pandemic started and, because we lack transportation as of late, we have scarcely left the apartment all year. A friend called at 11 a.m. inquiring whether our relationship survived, seeing as we are stuck together in this godforsaken apartment and must realize by now that even the littlest things can drive one to go insane . . . or to drink. But never with you. Never!

    I keep thinking about a time, not long after we met, when you took me to your childhood home. We drove down a dirt road to your trailer on the banks of Moenkopi Wash, its windows broken, boarded, and spray-painted in its abandonment. Sand jammed its cracks and coated the floor, peppered with broken glass and your belongings left miraculously in situ. We sat atop this now-barren arroyo, near the edge of your house, and you told me stories from your life here. "This is where I carried buckets of water," you said, because you had no running water inside. "This is where we watched the Moenkopi during monsoon season," when it ran crimson red. "Here is my old piano," where you taught yourself to play. "Here is where my telescope used to sit," and you remembered the dark skies that persuaded your passion for physics and astronomy.

    The whole day I kept thinking back to when I was a kid, saving my hard-earned cash for a story told by a respected keeper of traditional Diné medicine and oral history. Little did I know, then, that he was your grandfather. "We never teach our younger generation about these stories," he says. "I want you of the younger generation to learn these [songs and] stories and realize what they are for and to have you put it in your heads and remember it . . . I am giving my story so it will not fade. . . . We go by these songs; we live by these songs. . . . That is the way it is." Though I owned it for decades, I never ventured beyond its introduction, as his story was not mine to own, nor to read. And yet, as fate would have it, you and I found each other through our isolations. I can now return his story to you, threading the needle on his promise nearly seventy years in the making.

Now, that day is another memory to be told, nearly six years ago. Since then, we have shared much, burdened much. The Navajo Nation has become like a second home to me, because it is a part of you. It is a place where my skin seems to burn too quickly and where, in the mornings, we can jog on the banks of Pasture Canyon Reservoir accompanied by mallards, great blue herons, and pied-billed grebes with black stripes down their beaks as if duct-taped shut. And then, when our chests ache with fatigue and everything stings because it is worn raw with wind-blasted sand, we can return to your family, and we are welcome. We return and we are home.

I guess what I'm trying to say is that fate is a funny thing. Reading back through our story seems both impossible and inevitable. I am just grateful that, through it all, I have a partner with your grit, your wisdom, your talent, and your love.

That is the way it is.

—Jonathan

House of Aquilegia

If you came knocking at the door of a hanging garden, you might not recognize the desert that welcomes you inside. Vines slither through the trees, their leaves plump and heavy in the pocket of moisture. Nearby, carpets of moss weave like fine tapestries over sandstone and tree bark. Even the upwelling of water, fed by deep underground aquifers, attends a concert of moss, their funnel-like leaves upraised and swollen, basking in the rare gift of desert water.

Hanging gardens are, by definition, a contradiction. On my parent's property we had a garden where we planted potatoes, carrots, peppers, and squash beneath the limbs of our apple tree. We knew our plants as beings from underneath, sprouting upward to be harvested under the late-summer sun and fried in the sizzle of hot grease. I was disoriented by these gardens that inexplicably hung downward from alcove walls. It was as if roots had sprouted leaves and we were witnessing the curious event from the perspective of a burrowing prairie dog.

In their improbability, hanging gardens create a space of equally implausible biodiversity. Flora and fauna from wetland, riparian, and desert habitats join in these environments, establishing refuge for far more than plants. Birds, amphibians, insects, and mammals all bow deeply to the presence of water and shade.

My love of plants also took root in these spaces. It was often easy for me to miss the tiny yellow flowers of desert trumpets against the arid desert soils, but it was impossible to ignore jade-colored leaves laced over canyon walls. Deep in the darkness of hanging gardens, plumes of wildflowers sensitized me to the desert flora I had overlooked.

Alcove bog orchids, *Platanthera zothecina*, were one of those plants. Propped on slender stalks, bog orchid's rare flowers glimmer green, camouflaged among the dense vegetation. Once noticed, their flowers hang still like Wandjina: rain and clouds spirits from Australian Aboriginal stories. Wandjina are commonly painted on cliffs in tight compositions, some dating back thousands of years. Their faces tilt inquisitively with cosmic obsidian eyes and crimson crowns. Bog orchid flowers similarly cluster together, looking outward, their faces shaped by enclosed petals. According to stories, Wandjina foretell their deaths, painting their faces on the rocks before vanishing into a pool of water. It is believed they regenerate when their images are repainted. Much like bog orchids, the livelihoods of the Wandjina depend on finding these spaces of nourishment and seeding generations of caretakers.

On weekends, Aaron and I traveled far and wide to beloved hanging gardens in southern Utah, monitoring changes in vegetation and bloom times from respectful distances. We walked until blisters wore into our feet, scrambling through heart-stopping trails, pausing only to take notes for future sketches:

Alcove columbine, Aquilegia micrantha: *Its bone-white flowers look like ghosts swooping downward, arms against chests. The genus,* Aquilegia, *is derived from* aquila, *a Latin word for "eagle." Perhaps its flowers look like an eagle's thrashing claw. I prefer my pale, bobbing ghosts.*

Crimson monkeyflowers, Mimulus cardinalis: *Flowers with hair-tufted throats, the color of heartbreak. A provocative hummingbird seducer.*

I was prepared to discover many things in these gardens, but I never expected to find myself. It was near a hanging garden where I first questioned the church—a crack in my faith so fine that I could run my hands over it and feel nothing. Looking back, my belief was not a demolition. It was more like a cabin that stands in town for so long, no one thinks to check for rotting wood and missing bolts. It stays through wind and snow, and there is a time when you believe it will remain there forever. Then, one morning, you wake up and it is gone. But it would be foolish to say it was instantaneous. The collapse was preceded by years of blind eyes and a witless belief that checking in would somehow manifest the inevitable, as if by not observing its integrity, it would stay there in diapause.

It may come as a surprise, or no surprise at all, that the first crack was not my sexuality. It was a cottontail. A rabbit. I had a shotgun in my hands, breathing slowly, air clear and empty in the middle of February. I was old enough to hunt with a church leader, or so I was told, and we spent hours crossing grassland and sage, passing muffin-topped sandstone and junipers stripped naked against the turquoise sky. This was an honor in my community, a coming of age when boys became men. I couldn't rationalize my discomforts, both for the rabbit and my uncertainty regarding gender, so I sat on the rim of an arroyo, watching it breathe. I saw its button eyes and sensed the vibration of its pulse. I stared until its tiny heartbeat became my own. Clenching my eyes shut, I did what I knew I would never do again, and I pulled the trigger.

It fired. I missed, intentionally, and the church leader noted my loss of motivation. "Animals are placed here on this planet for our consumption," he growled, eyebrows snapped together. "We do with them whatever we want!"

I felt guilty, somehow, that it bothered me. I lacked the words, and emotional capability, to express my discontent. After all, I was a child to a long line of hunters and, while I did not share their desires, I saw in them an appreciation of the animal. They were people that found no dissonance between living creatures and the meat on their plates. It was a form of gratitude I did not fully understand as a vegetarian, but could nonetheless respect. But here was a man with a lust to kill, having no use nor purpose for the life he was taking.

Seven words can blemish faith: *we do with them whatever we want*. I memorized it, deconstructed it, and my youth was filled with firm reconciliations. I assumed that it was a misunderstanding, an err in translation, until I found him harassing snakes for humor, to show around his workplace for laughs and a brand of machismo that fills me with bitter rage. I believed his words. I believed his actions. I thought *I* was wrong and weak for disobeying someone holy.

Turquoise Messengers

During an unseasonably dry year in an even drier season, it is raining. Denizens of the Sonoran Desert hang on to words like incantations—*drought, climate change, wildfires*—yet their appetite for expansion bears an ominous resemblance to post-apocalyptic horror films. Then there are the long-term residents of Sonora, people who remember the past and warn of the ever-warming climate: the cacophonous toads that used to be, biblical-scale floods that once were, riverbeds now dry enough for the young pharaoh Tutankhamun to hunt in an oxen-towed chariot.

I walk through the desert each evening—or what passes for desert in urban Tucson. Here there are palo verde trees and islands of sago palms cultivated in open fields, each about fifteen feet in height. Ornate tree lizards attempt to camouflage on the trunks of orange trees on street sides, made conspicuous by their zestful push-ups, but finding more effective cover in granite transplanted from the Catalina Mountains. Then there are the swimming pools dotting the landscape in defiance of Tucson's water shortages, trimmed with fat crimson hibiscus flowers. Here, between water and sky, there is an unnatural shade of blue—I've come to call it Urban Sonora Blue—that frames each evening.

There is a swimming pool not far from my apartment, bordered on its long edges with stout bushes with wine-colored blossoms. Feathery leaves drape downward to the water, creating an illusion of wildness among a jungle of concrete and stucco. I tease its surface with my feet, tempted by its unexpected coolness, but I shouldn't enter, I think, because entering would make me complicit. A little destruction ad infinitum that bleeds Sonora dry. Cicadas cling to the poolside branches, shrilling desperately in the heat and humidity, until they stretch their arms and give up on life, dropping to the cement back-first and cadaverous. Understandable given the weather. I consider joining them, splayed against the ground, soon to be mummified by intense cosmic rays. It was almost unbearable, enough atmospheric moisture to boil me alive, but not enough to supply the exhausted aquifers deep beneath Sonora. *I shouldn't enter.*

Sweat drips from my brow and I yield to the pool's devilish invitation, walking until I am forced to swim, arms spread outward, trailing my fingers against the deep end until I rise for oxygen. I come back every day, feeling my protest-by-abstinence turn sharply toward refuge. It is utterly empty, a deserted plot of turquoise surrendered to vegetation, so covered in leaves one quickly loses sight of its surface.

Nearby, tanning chairs lie vacant, most of them sun-bleached into faint, earth-toned barred and geometric shapes. On their fabric, layers of dust and pinacate beetle corpses hint at abandonment. The pool hadn't been used for months, if not years, but I found this reticence and air of secrecy more remedying than ominous. I am told that some people, those adapted to these strange sanctuaries of human populations called cities or—God forbid—metropolises, find silence to be an unsettling absence, but I have grown fond of hearing the faithful thrum of my heartbeat, reminding me that I am still vigilant and alive, and shaped by the careful arrangement of desert and star stuff. This, I believe, is abundance.

As the weeks march onward without rainfall, I observe a marked shift in animals' behavior. They edge closer to the pool, and tiptoe toward the city. They chew through water caches intended for lost migrants arriving from Mexico.

Today, I find a lizard that crushes me. She is partially submerged in the pool, arms stooped and lifeless. The walls provided her entry but were too steep and slick for her little feet to grasp. I jump in the pool and cusp her body in my palms, swimming her to a bed of dried leaves. She curls and freezes. Her eyes turn glassy and transfixed. I try to coax her along by rubbing her belly, finding it smooth like velvet against fingertips, but her body feels woefully uninhabited.

I have never felt heartbreak so sudden and painful. I have lost people and loved ones, but never had I felt death in my hands. There is a human cognizance of death that makes it easier for me to endure. We may fear it, deny it, but we always bear the realization that it comes for everyone and when it arrives, we must accept it. I believe everyone I have loved and lost met peace before death. But it is the lizard's fear and confusion that eviscerates me, the brittleness of innocent death.

I stare at her transfixed, how her delicate black stripes reveal the cosmos of the desert—the stark striations of granite, the fine grains of color-shifting sand, a sereness confessed in her body like a love letter to Sonora. I stroke her head one last time to memorize the geography of her scales, but I sense something deeper. I feel her body lifted in deep, billowy breaths. Her eyes flick open. She scampers to the overgrowth and dives head-first into the desert.

During an unseasonably dry year in an even drier season, it is raining.

But it is raining ash.

Her home is on fire. North of Tucson, a cloud of smoke conceals the Catalina Mountains. The sun is red, the air apocalyptic. Flames sizzle behind a forest of saguaros. Gila woodpeckers stare from their crests in awe and shock. Thick puffs of ash fall upon the city, burned bodies of old trees and little creatures.

Her family may be among the deceased, flickering the sky like a deadly canopy of stars.

In these moments, I want nothing more than to strip my humanity, to feel the earth beneath the pads of my feet. I wish to make a vow beyond words as if I am not complicit. I remind myself that society leaves us few choices: everything is shrink-wrapped, exploited, milked until it is not only dry but destitute, but I'd rather grieve with them, stake my alliances. I want to feel that there is more to my societal disconnects than grief and intolerance, as if I could wake up to scales, or wings, or any confirmation that I wasn't human at all. That would be easy. What is hard is to live and not belong.

But today I am in a pool, ten feet down, looking up through currents streaked like oil paint. A streetlight breaks over the surface, shifting as the water laps to the sides. Leaves pirouette down, as does ash. Honeybees seek refuge, diving to the pool, standing on a film of water before they, too, sink. I pluck them out one by one, feeling balls of fuzz squirming in my palms, placing them where it is warm and dry. They twitch their soaked bodies, combing their legs over their heads, leaving damp trails where their sternum drags against the cement. Many survive. Many do not, circling the pool's graveyard in sunny specks.

I emerge from the pool and the desert creatures follow, thinking my blue trunks are the closest prayer to real water. I mourn for them, leaving a basin in front of my door, a drink for these weathered beings. But it is not enough. I worry nothing ever will be. I apologize as they march behind me, knowing they can't understand a word. Maybe I do it for myself. Guilt is a brittle thing. When they break, I break with them.

—

In my parents' yard is a weeping willow. It was my favorite place to be when it rained. It owes its name to its grief-stricken appearance as water swells on its upper branches, falling like tear drops. We grieved together as I curled my legs around its lower branches, reading Ellen Meloy's *The Anthropology of Turquoise*, whose pages remained dry beneath the cover of leaves. "Everyone will tell you that genealogy serves two purposes: self-knowledge and social status," she writes, "some sort of pedigree divined from names, locations, and achievements of eminence. However, there is nothing quite like an anomaly to suck attention away from the droning census records. A suicide hinted at emotion and thought. A closet door was flung open and daylight flooded a skeleton."

A skeleton. At the time, I still identified as Mormon, and a faithful one at that. But I would be remiss to suggest I was anything more than a thorn in my heritage, with a feeling of unbelonging that was never balanced by faith. I was the bag of bones, arid and bleached, spread out and disassembled, but also one step closer to freedom. Unbound from the ligaments of my past.

I came back to this willow when California introduced Proposition 8 in 2008, a bill that would outlaw same-sex marriage in California. Church leaders called upon its members to lend their personal time and finances to the cause, joined with the full might of the church's funds and resources. Our families were asked to campaign against us. We were asked to campaign against ourselves. The actions of the church divided the very families they professed to uphold.

The bill passed.

Same-sex marriage was illegal.*

"I am not for this world," I wrote in the aftermath. "Either I am in the wrong time, or I am in the wrong body, or both, but the feeling is all the same."

But here I was, thirteen years old, not sure of myself. Not sure of what to make of these feelings. Was I gay? Could that change? I felt this death, believing it to be my own. So much of

---

* This was later overturned by federal courts in California. Same-sex marriage became legal nationwide seven years later.

my personality was bound to my faith. If I was gay, the church must not be true, and if the church was not true, neither was I. There was no existence beyond white gowns and sacrament hymns, or warm evenings with the Book of Mormon beside wood crackle in the fireplace.

Losing faith was like a zipper clenched shut on a thick plastic body bag. There is something familiar inside, but it is cold, strangely vacant, and grief and memory are intertwined. Loved ones come to grieve, to plead and to bargain, but they know something wretched and final has come. Then they move on, eventually, with swollen eyes and twisted fists, and life returns with or without you.

In Mormonism, spiritual death is worse than physical death, and both leave you with an empty shell of a body. Do you curse now? Drink tea? Wear normal underwear? You fall back into a world estranged from you, or you from it, but it hardly matters. Everything is autonomous. You are greeted by faceless employees in stores. They say something about faith, some purportedly uplifting statement, a skeleton from their own past they wrangled back into its lifeless corpse, but you tone it out. You aren't going back. Your family is a blur, muttering in hushed tones, their eyes flickering in your direction. You know they speak of you, but it doesn't matter. Little does. Everything is empty and mindless, a trickle of memory blotted out in heartbreak.

I did what I knew best and consulted with this fierce spirit, Ellen Meloy. She had passed just four years prior. Her books now lined my shelf like an altar, placed among sticks and brambles from my home. A vial of sand from the Pacific Ocean stood beyond them. She spoke, through my youth, the closest thing to an honest testimony.

"Of all the things I wondered about on this land," she wrote, "I wondered the hardest about the seduction of certain geographies that feel like home—not by story or blood but merely by their forms and colors. How our perceptions are our only internal map of the world, how there are places that claim you and places that warn you away. How you can fall in love with the light."

Like an answer to my prayerful consultations, her paragraph was cut short by pattering wings—a blur of turquoise, a blink of lace, a head sparkling like broken glass. It was a dragonfly, a species dependent on creek water and river cobble, sojourned so far from his usual haunts to visit me here. He swiveled and swerved through our humble farmlands before arriving back to my perch, hovering just a few inches from my face. We stared at each other long in pollen-colored light until he departed toward the river, making his distant journey back home. But he came back, and he came back often. I made a vow, a promise from within these jumbled bones, to honor his form.

In my past and present, I have known his shape to be divine, a double-barred cross, yielding the potential for simplicity, while remaining indecipherable to anything short of micro-scopic vision. It is pecked and painted in sandstone sanctuar-ies in the Bears Ears among tawny handprints and figures with carved slit eyes and bell-shaped jewelry. In the New World, it accompanied Jesuit missionaries to represent Jesus of Nazareth's crucifixion, exploiting his sacred image to compel Indigenous people into the Christian faith, whether by intention or coin-cidence. False promises were made, coyote grins were had, but nothing managed to diminish his power.

His form is carried on my bloodline, a love passed down by maternal women, disciples of his mysticism and elegance, and then to me. When my mother passes, she vows to return as a dragonfly, defying gender and doctrine to carry the color of a robin's egg—a color often appearing only on males. This shape, a map of family and riparian desert, has never left my side. I find his silhouette printed on oven mitts and towels, on blankets and sheets. I do not ask for these things. I do not buy them. They find me wherever I go. Some of them were in my apartment when I moved in, others were gifts from Aaron's family, unaware of the personal significance. I found his image plastered on the walls of friends' houses, none of them entirely sure where he came from. He was "just there," as if his image was passed down, hand to hand, over generations. Gifts from the women of my past.

And then I met R. E. Burrillo.

He is an archaeologist and fellow vagabond whom I met while photographing the Bears Ears National Monument at the behest of tribal and conservation groups. He bears a tattoo of a dragonfly, wings fine-edged and geometric, outspread on his upper arm.

"I got this after being diagnosed with Lyme disease," he said. "I once wrote a short story expressing my confusion that I made it through my own traumatic childhood without successfully ending it all. It's what the dragonfly symbolizes."

When he got sick, a dragonfly landed on his hand, missing a leg but moving freely. He was sky blue, like mine, with a cross-bone pattern through his wings. This tattoo was a memory as much as it was a message, and we were both recipients, finding hope and kinship in uncommon encounters.

What did it mean to feel so close to a creature when humanity felt so distant? I have been told that our connection to the wild is a relationship of destruction—by boots that erode the soil, by cars that spit smoke, by heaps of trash that litter nearly every street corner. What if animals care for me as I care for them? I can't shed responsibility for human encroachment as if destruction is an inevitable state of human existence, encoded in DNA like hair color or a predisposition to ailments. I must love to reciprocate. I must feel to change. The climate, like identity, is part of everyone's responsibility. I believe it is tenderness, strong relationships, and earnest humility that will bring a better end to humanity's tumultuous roads. Listen to your messengers, match their generosity, partake in a world where humans love and care for the planet, because they are a part of it.

Double-Headed Passerine

It is my eleventh birthday and my father is taking my brothers and me through a blizzard on the flanks of the Colorado Plateau. I am tucked in a gaudy white Cabela's coat, mismatched camouflage gloves, and an orange balaclava cinched over my windburned nose. The rest of my family is wearing too-tight camouflage jumpsuits, waddling in a line against the sandstone. Behind us, there are fences spray-painted red, posted with signs that warn that this "Private Land [is] Defended by Government Surveillance Drones. Enter at your own risk." We have permission to enter. We are not blasted to smithereens by definitely-not-fictional, top-secret laser beams.

Near the fence, we find fat paw prints pressed in the snow, glimpsing its trail through our frozen eyelashes: wide hind pads, distinctly clawless. My father bends down to examine the tracks, identifying them with gravitas.

"Puma!"

They are accompanied by boot prints, someone who walked through the arroyo moments before we arrived, parking their snowmobile at the trunk of an old cottonwood. We follow the prints into the canyon until we find the guy: a lumberjack-looking man with a stiff, farmer-build musculature and an all plaid getup. Short ginger hairs poke out from underneath a woolen cap, framing his round, stocky face. Snow has accumulated in his wild facial hair, concealing any gray hairs that may have turned.

"Yeah, I'm tryin' to chase down the cat," he says, adjusting his overcoat. "I gave up my gun for a camera. I get more shots this way."

He lumbers over to me, bending down to look into my elusive eyeballs. "Your dad tells me you're a birthday boy. Happy birthday, Jonathan!"

I don't respond. I'm not sure why. It's like I'm caught in one of those dreams where you lose your faculties. I search my mind, wipe off the dust bunnies operating my frontal lobe with pert little paws, but feel there is absolutely no appropriate response to this flummoxing statement. My father ushers him over and whispers out of earshot. I miss most of their conversation but eavesdrop on three words: *awkward, quiet, impaired.*

This memory was filed away somewhere in a mental closet, nearly forgotten, until I met with a doctor. I decided the only way to decode this vagrant brain was to make a list of my failed behaviors. I titled it: My Lack of Sense and Sensibilities. I assumed Jane Austen would approve. After much discussion, the doctor returned with their scary "diagnoses"—an informal professional opinion until I was willing to cough up a small fortune and get an evaluation with lab-rat scrutiny. I declined. Meanwhile, I was told I likely had ASD and possibly ADHD. So many letters I became distracted by their potential to yield me a Scrabble advantage. They zeroed in on ASD, autism spectrum disorder.

The National Institute of Mental Health describes ASD as "a developmental disorder that affects communication and behavior. Although autism can be diagnosed at any age, it is said to be a 'developmental disorder' because symptoms generally appear in the first two years of life." Signs and symptoms include lack of eye contact, difficulty socializing, anxiety, narrow interests, sensory issues, and a tendency for list-making.

Shit.

"What you need, Jonathan," they said, "is a support network.

Maybe some other people on the autism spectrum. Some breathing exercises. That could do a lot of good for you."

I explained that I did have a support network. I just needed them to waddle down from their rocky perches, as I lacked their gravity-defying hooves.

"Not sheep, Jonathan . . . fellow humans."

I most certainly hated the sound of that. At Aaron's behest, I begrudgingly agreed to meet a few people, somehow getting the idea that they should be *gay* people. Lacking the means to do so in a new city, Aaron signed me up for a dating app designed for casual hookups and moral ambiguity. Beneath my profile picture was a tagline which read, "Let's talk about sheep. P.S. I'm unavailable." Most assumed it was an innuendo involving horns, after which I changed it to "Let's talk about ungulates. P.S. I'm unavailable."

Those who realized I was seeking platonic compadres were often determined to nurture me into my gay-hood, with an itinerary for my metamorphosis:

Get him into full makeup.

Attend a drag show, in drag.

Perform on karaoke night.

I refused their generous offers, but noted that a recording of their karaoke night would do well to attract mountain lions.

—

Losing faith in the church requires you to reconsider your perception of identity. It's more like a head-on collision. You take that wreckage and you make a new person out of it. You take the warped metal, broken glass, and the steering wheel, and shape it into a self that feels safe and familiar. In my case, whatever Scrabble tiles specialists use to define my dust-bunny brain, the person I became is influenced by more than sexual identity. He is shaped by love, wilderness, trauma, and neurological handicaps.

Acceptance, I found, was easier to seek than understanding.

In all their warmth, LGBTQ+ spaces are often cast in a particular mold, a mold that does not extend to people who are fundamentally, radically different than the stereotype of who we, as queer people, are expected to be. I don't particularly mind the expectations, as they mean very little to me while accompanying seemingly helium-filled sheep or my lesbian lizard comrades, *Aspidoscelis neomexicanus*—an all-female species of whiptail that reproduce asexually, but still copulate female-on-female to aid ovulation. I would rather listen to the yearning of hungry eaglets in scarlet cliffs than to music with bass-heavy rumblings that feel like a trespass on my psyche—dust bunnies rattled off the frontal lobe.

Whatever you sculpt from the loss of faith, or in the revelation of sexual identity, is valid. "I am a rare species, not a stereotype," writes LGBTQ+ activist Ivan Coyote. The paths we take are ours to travel, or not travel. We may stay transfixed at one point on our perceived destination, finding more joy and comfort in watching the world move around us. That is our decision, our personal authority in action.

I am not concerned about being accepted or understood. I have made an indivisible bond with fur, feathers, and scales—creatures which seem strangely more human to me than bipedal hominids with peculiar social protocols that serve neither curiosity nor utility. "It is not socially acceptable to open a conversation with sheep facts," says Aaron. But how else will one know how a well-endowed ram courts a ewe in estrous while shuffling his manly hips?

I am concerned for other people, those of us whose queerness exceeds their sexual or gender identity. They have traveled far from solitude to find themselves on the margins of their own clan, lacking words that give meaning to their heartache. Maybe they will think that they have lived too wild, occupied spaces too large, or befriended species too solitary and mystifying. Maybe they will think of Darwin's finches and wonder if they are not just adapted to a different island, but quite genetically flawed—a two-headed passerine, so to speak.

Representation is one remedy. One may think of movies, or books, or big-wig CEOs, but it really begins in hearts and dialogue.

"I realize that the English language is sadly devoid of names for people like me," Ivan Coyote continues. "I try to cut the world some slack for this every day. All day. And the day after that, too. But the truth is that . . . a tiny little sliver of me disappears, a tiny little sliver of me is reminded that I do not fit. I remember that the truth of me is invisible, and a tiny little sliver of me disappears. . . . All those slivers add up to something much harder to pretend around."

—

Fifteen years after my eleventh birthday and I am in an apartment, writing as the pandemic spirals out of control. The newspapers report that Tucson has creeped a hair's length from one hundred thousand cases—nearly 10 percent of the population by 2021. I put the paper aside and lift a photograph from my desk. The image reveals a boy with a roundish face, buzzed blond hair, and a look of discontent. I often wonder what he would think if he were to peer through my eyes today. He would find himself in a foreign place, near a bookshelf stuffed with titles most assuredly forbidden: *¡Tequila!: Distilling the Spirit of Mexico*, *The Sixth Extinction*, *Your Inner Fish*. He would see a version of himself that is older, much slimmer, with fine wrinkles budding on his cheeks and forehead. His eyes, inexplicably, a little more nebulous in their ashen blue. He would see his boyfriend in an armchair, wrapped in a gray Pendleton scarf, with a cup of coffee in his hands. Masked pedestrians would pass by the windows. What would he think of them?

I am holding a photograph of a boy who is eleven years old and terrified of this life for which he lacks the vocabulary to explain. His present, I think, may be as difficult to conceptualize as his future. I won't tell him of the noose raised at the nearest LGBTQ+ club, or the man whose jaw was broken because he showed affection to his partner on Fourth Avenue. I won't tell him he was called a faggot when he decided it was safe to wear pride clothing amid this new city in southern Arizona. I won't tell him many things about his sexuality and disability, and ever do I wonder when we can both stop pretending.

Journal Entry: January 16, 2021

In disability,
life is porcelain.
I feel its cracks
beneath my fingertips.

And all that's left
is all I could hold
and my hands
know this fragile truth.

That I hold tight
to what I must
because everything else
will fall apart.

From thirty thousand feet, the Sonoran Desert becomes a patchwork of color. Below the plane, I can see only shadowy toothpicks: thirty-foot-tall saguaros stretching nearly to the horizon, T-posing through shapeless boundaries between color and shade. I am reminded of my early years as a painter when I was more concerned about freedom than creation, dipping my hands in acrylic, stroking my fingertips over scraps of linen. It was a heavy-handed approach to evoke the geological processes of the Colorado Plateau, carving deep, abstract canyons from underneath my thumb. The Sonoran Desert, by contrast, would have required a far more delicate process, or less intention, a haphazardness that spills the watercolor pallet, sending pigment deep underground, leaving only pastel tones on its surface.

From above, I witness the ghosts of the Sonoran Desert, where time and history reduce to formlessness. That canyons, peaks, and rivers dwelled beneath this sheen was simply unfathomable to me. But in this desert, time reveals itself similarly, with broader pasts matched by blurrier perspectives.

—

Cucurbita foetidissima, coyote gourd, is a plant with small, watermelon-looking fruit plopped below low, sprawling leaves more representative of a community garden than a desert expanse. It is a xerophyte, like cacti, meaning that it has adapted to live in an environment with little available water.

I became enamored with this species shortly after spotting it in the back pages of a field guide. I'm not sure what it was—the little non-watermelons, the adorably heart-shaped leaves, or the fact it was one of the few gourds native to the Southwest. I simply had to meet these new fruit comrades, certain we were destined to become close friends.

Aaron and I got in our Jeep and drove over five hundred miles to an area I was told to be prime habitat for coyote gourds, but the area didn't jive with my imaginings. From my experience growing gourds, they were notoriously finicky, struggling to live in nutrient-rich, loamy soils saturated with cow manure from our friendly neighborhood farmers. Aaron had a similar experience trying to bring, well, much of anything to life in the sandy plains of the Navajo Nation. So, I assumed a mistake had been made when we drove up to a sparsely vegetated mesa with drifting sand and chaparral thorn-scapes, looking for a plant whose relatives in the family Cucurbitaceae were known to me as fickle beings.

But find it we did, in a sandy floodplain, isolated from the more vegetated slopes below the cliffs. We hopped out. We took photos. I felt like I was returning from a long-estranged friendship, doing my best to refrain from embracing the plant, certain that my title of tree-hugger would be demoted to the allegedly worse gourd-hugger.

But something felt missing, as if we'd been fooled into a second of a plant whose history was truly timeless. As author Connie Barlow put it, it was like I was witnessing a ghost. That missing ingredient, as it turns out, was megafauna.

—

Around ten thousand years ago—virtually yesterday in geologic terms, but a *long time ago* from our fragile human perspective—the world was leaving the Ice Age. As glaciers melted and the earth warmed, large mammals over one hundred pounds, or megafauna, became extinct through North America. Other parts of the world would experience similar extinctions, although not necessarily simultaneously, and for reasons that are still up for debate, Africa was largely spared of its elephants, giraffes, hippos, and everything else poaching and climate change is trying to have another go at. While leading factors for this zoological impoverishment are still unsettled—whether climate change, arriving human populations, cataclysmic events, disease, alien death rays to make room for intergalactic sasquatches—the consequences are the same.* In North America, mammoths, mastodons, American horses, ancient bison, camelids, dire wolves, western turtles, and ground sloths were all among the casualties.

The key here is adaptation, and flora and fauna had been doing that long before megafauna were sent to their dusty graves. As seen with one of my favorite winged companions, the yucca moth—its wings so silken and white one tends to see them as purple—that has coevolved with specific species of yucca, plants adapted to megafauna because they coexisted and coevolved long before our current geological epoch. When megafauna

---

* The Quaternary extinction event ended with the demise of many species of animals, particularly megafauna. Some researchers have proposed that people arriving in North America hunted megafauna to extinction, interrupting the ecological balance and leading to the decline of other species. Another hypothesis suggests that climate change, as temperatures warmed and glaciers melted, could have forced animals to occupy environments in which they were not adapted to survive. Other hypotheses point to a meteor impact or infectious diseases as potential causes, though these hypotheses are not without flaws. Megafauna extinctions throughout the world were not simultaneous. Australian megafauna, for example, became extinct about forty thousand years ago. This is in keeping with the overkill hypothesis, as humans originated in Africa where they would have adapted with the megafauna, then spread into Eurasia, Australia, the Americas, and outlier islands at different times. However, if the demise of megafauna had been caused by a singular cataclysmic event (like a meteor) these staggered extinctions would seem unlikely. But if humans were responsible for the extinction of megafauna, the evidence is sparse. Few species seem to have been hunted and examples of human predation are slim pickings. In the case of climate change, shifts in temperature and ice were not unprecedented and, in some circumstances, large mammals survived conditions worse than that of the last Ice Age. It is probable that a combination of these hypotheses contributed to the extinction of megafauna at the end of the Pleistocene, perhaps with climate change leading the way.

became extinct, not all of their adaptive partners went extinct with them. In some cases, plant species found other, sometimes disproportionately expensive, means of propagating. These species, stripped of their beloved partners, are known as evolutionary anachronisms—anachronism coming from the Greek words *ana* and *kronos*, translating to "against time." For example, my nephews remind me that compact discs are now an anachronism shortly before inquiring if they can rob me of my camera because I won't be needing it much longer, given my advanced age of twenty-six.

In the case of our coyote gourd, these thick-skinned fruits may have been munched by the likes of mammoths: American horses—those native to North America, not the horses that arrived with the Spanish invasion—and camels, which are not only native to North America, but *originated* here, traveling across the Bering Land Bridge connecting present-day Asia and North America, then progressing further south nearer to where they are found today. Some of these camels, not feeling the journey northward, evolved into alpacas and llamas in South America.

After these seeds passed through the stomachs of now-extinct animals, they were deposited in places where they might be able to grow, complete with a nutritious, steaming fertilizer. As these species vanished to time, no surviving animals had adapted to the plant, and propagating future populations proved to be challenging—whether from selective pressures or heartbreak, I can't be too sure.

Today, coyote gourd is ruthlessly bitter despite its delectable-looking fruit, hence its name—coyote being the trickster that, according to the O'odham people, deceitfully planted the distasteful plant in his scat. Though, when young, the fruits are edible, and Indigenous people have consumed them for millennia, along with the gourd's protein-rich seeds after roasting or boiling.

There have also been reports of collared peccaries (javelinas) eating the fruit, though it has yet to be seen whether its seeds survive the peccaries' fervid chewing and digestive system. But this observation is historically inconsequential, given that flat-headed peccaries, *Platygonus compressus*, went extinct about 11,500 years ago. What are known today as javelinas, *Dicotyles tajuca*, are recent arrivals from the south, perhaps occupying their present range as recently as the last few hundred years. To put it plainly, coyote gourds experienced a significant gap without peccaries, thus needing to find other means of propagation.

With or without coyote gourds, there are many other evolutionary anachronisms—a few of which are probably in your fridge right now. Think avocados or mangos, whose seeds are far too large for existing animals to gobble down (although humans now kindly do their bidding), but would have been no problem for, say, a giant sloth or the elephant-like Gomphothere. In the Southwest, there exist several anachronistic plants, like *Cylindropuntia fulgida*—jumping cholla, a cactus whose fruit frequently dries out before it can be consumed by present-day animals. (Being a stabby asshole also does not compel much temptation.) Another is *Opuntia ficus-indica*, also known as prickly pear cactus, Barbary fig, or nopal. Not to be confused with its miniature cousin that shares its name, this prickly pear can reach fifteen feet in height with blush ping-pong-ball fruits. Megafauna may have played a significant role in nopal seed dispersal as its spines are higher than present-day browsers.

Ultimately, when you encounter these plants that exist "against time," you may see them as living relics, or you may see them as ghosts, but it is most important to see them as memories of the desert's deep time, reminding us of the delicate web that threads together living beings. Writer Robin Wall Kimmerer would call this "land reciprocity"—an eternal cycle of reliance, gratitude, and contribution. As monocultures and human-caused climate change create a vanishing world of biodiversity, remember these "ghosts," the reliant partners who mourn the downfall of great species. Else we become ghost-makers, we must partake in this reciprocity, taking only what we can give back.

Time Travelers of a Different Eukaryote

A zucchini squash sits on the table. The youngest of my older brothers brought it from the garden, flexing it in his hands to check its firm-but-not-too-firm ripeness. He placed it in front of me while flicking on the stove, waiting patiently with one hand on his hip, the other clutching a jar of Crisco. Meanwhile, I am transfixed by its swamp-green skin, conjuring thoughts of obese bullfrogs—not-so-little *Lithobates*, who look like gluttony made manifest: elliptic zucchini with round, bulging eyes as if protruded by a squeeze of their inflated white bellies. In the swamps near our house—a wetland refuge of alfalfa and burst irrigation pipes—I always expected them to hop from under the thicket donning top hats, perhaps a monocle, a gold chain worth more than our entire township. They looked as expensive as they were invasive—a species that demands to be greeted by its full Latin name, *Lithobates catesbeianus*—hitching rides into the region under the guise of fish bait and small-game targets. A small price to pay for global domination. Here they choke out native species, occupy marshes and waterways—push, proceed, conquer. It was a matter of time, I thought, before I bowed down to our bullfrog overlords, grown so large and portly, they flick turkey vultures from the sky with their whip-like tongues. For now, they squat between reeds, looking about as smug and self-centered as Gucci-studded Angelenos. When the right moment comes—whatever their alarm—they shrill like an injured parakeet and leap into shallows with a dull thunk.

My brother takes the zucchini and cuts it on the bias, slicing it into smaller helpings. I try to lose my thoughts of bullfrogs as he snaps the knife through the vegetable's hard outer flesh, sliding it into the pan with a flick of the blade. My mind fails to persuade as I stare at the greenish fillets in silent horror, watching them scream in hot grease—a sound so high-pitched and unnerving, I question whether my eyes had summoned a squash where a fat bullfrog was surely butchered. To eat or not to eat, that is the question my grumbling stomach wanted not to answer. With the pouring of whipped egg, he silences the yowling under a curtain of thick, silken yolk.

Breakfast is served.

My parents are up north, a two-hour drive to the nearest specialist for my father's biennial visit to the doctor. Two Boeing 767s have crashed into the World Trade Center, but I am blissfully unaware, gulping down my fare of scrambled eggs and squash. Or is it bullfrog? The television is shut off, no one has called, and the town is eerily silent. In households throughout Ferron—little to our knowledge—emotions are running high. In the days that follow, panicked rumors circulate around town— whispers of Muslim takeover, gay agendas, the nefarious plot of a liberal elite to take down our all-too-self-destructive power plants. One teacher, many years later, announces to the class that the takeover has reached its apex—a traitorous, Muslim terrorist (read: Obama) has overtaken the presidency.

One thinks of bigotry, racism, homophobia, yet this September morning revealed a deeper kernel. Ellen Meloy, my oft-quoted guide with whom I share a disincarnate kinship, writes: "The American West has always been adept at 'otherizing.' These days people who see a familiar world disrupted . . . want to blame someone for the erosion of rural simplicity, for the cracks in the old ways, be they mythical or real. . . . Wariness of outsiders, fear of change and a sense of powerlessness in the face of it—fear, in fact, of the rest of the world—have bred a convenient duplicity of perpetrator and victim and an unwholesome battery of revenge politics."

What I missed, somehow, was how fearful my community had become—fear of people moving in, fear of people moving out; fear of new businesses opening and beloved businesses closing down; fear of expanding the population and a fear—as woeful as it may be—of watching the community and its traditions waltz steadily toward extinction. They feared becoming the next Moab—believed to be the recreation hub for hippies, junkies, the effeminately inclined unmentionables, the government, and liberal plotters wringing their hands on rural gentrification—pining for a past that never existed. A few residents still insisted on living in underground bunkers marooned from the Cold War and did not appreciate me inquiring if tubers grew from their ceilings—certain that death, communism, and end-times lie on the near horizon. If my community took charge of the Doctor's Tardis, I thought, they may well refuse all of time and space to freeze history somewhere around 1950, when times were simpler and therefore *better*.

If you look beyond their anti-otherness behavior—which results in more worldly participation than I think they truly desire—there is something quite melancholic in these anachronistic communities fated to exist decades in the past, each person raised to hold tight to something desired and long gone, fearing, more than hating, the world around them. Urbanites—Ferron's idea of an invasive species—often see the rural folk as zealous brutes, dragging down the country with taxpayer subsidized farms (the goods of which they gobble down with belch-inducing feasts), and with asymmetrical political clout due in no small part to the Electoral College. They believe, it seems, that rural communities are populated by the uneducated, the short-sighted, or the willfully evil. Both politics come with more entrenchment than long-term solutions.

My brother—I think now he had learned of the attacks but

said nothing—rests his hand on my shoulder and tells me that today is deserving of a walk. We travel to the Molen Reef under a royal-blue sky—a color which I expect to be worn by our tyrannical frogs, but is not—and drive to a gravel lot curiously lacking visitors. We walk until the wind nips our fingers, visiting ancient figures pecked in brown-red patina: owls, fanged creatures, a figure tanning an ambiguous animal hide. Another figure—penis raised in the spirit of fecundity or in excitement for game animals—lifts an atlatl toward a bighorn ram. In this solitude, we have escaped with our spirits full and hearts intact.

—

Nearly two decades after the attacks on the World Trade Center, a mob breaks into the United States Capitol, hoping to prevent the certified victory of Joseph R. Biden as president of the United States. They come with zip-tie cuffs, weapons, and—if their chants are to be taken seriously—the will to take members of the political class captive while erecting a noose to hang our current vice president. Assassinations on live television. One person, donning Romanesque armor, swivels a flag emblazoned with a quote from Moroni—the last prophet of a group (the Nephites) in the Book of Mormon to descend from Nephi, a prophet who allegedly left Jerusalem for the Americas around 600 BC. It reads: "In memory of our God, our religion, and freedom, and our peace, our wives, and our children."

His example stands not as a comparison between the violent mob and Mormon faith. Rather, it demonstrates the parallels between far-right extremists and western ideologies: the fierce fortification of the heterosexual family unit, the erosion of a simple past that has slipped hopelessly through their fingers, the burden of urbanites and political correctness, and, mostly, their shared contempt for the federal government. The scary others, if you will.

The fertile soils from which extremist ideologies sprout

run far, far deeper than any election. Perhaps it is an exploitation of some immutable human feature, encoded somewhere in the human genome next to toolmaking and our proclivity for sharing memes. Hijacking these desires, our need for kinship in a lonely, industrialized era is risky business. Social media has driven so much engagement and milked so much of our psyche, my platforms have already decided my dinner menu, my wardrobe, and observed my ravenous downing of a cookie platter and recommends a thorough test for diabetes. I no longer must wonder what this makes of people hungry for violence, macerated by hatred of the "lesser others," or simply deserted in a social bubble of little diversity—be it real or online.

In online social worlds, all users curate bubbles as they see fit—unfriending, blocking, reaching out to political opposites only when a camera follows behind, hoping to expose their otherness, to feed online followers created in the absence of real kinship. Users are encouraged to burn every bridge at the slightest signal of free thought, forgetting that every arsonist's dream will prohibit progress on both sides. Social media giants, in turn, feed content that keeps people scrolling; content that rips and tears at the democratic fabric and family bonds, devalues humans as conscious beings, and affirms any conspiracies they have predisposed.

These days, it is radical to be kind. Some of my friends tell me they see value in it, but couldn't participate in such undeserved and radical acts. Others accuse the sentiment as complicity with sexism, homophobia, racism, and the pothole they hit while fuming over my Facebook status. I ask them to rethink what it means to be kind—often to no avail. Kindness is not earned nor deserved, it is a choice much like my refraining from streaking through supermarket aisles—a conscious decision for the betterment of society. Another friend, who I regularly confide in to jumpstart this dust-bunny brain, said that far-right ideologies are like a troll under the bridge—you can't defeat it until it comes into the light. I asked if they ever considered why such an angry troll loomed under the bridge. What makes a troll a troll?

The uncomfortable truth is that my means of engagement, rather than the beliefs I hold, must say more about the world I wish to live in. The way I treat people does not pardon their behavior, it is a lifeline to pull them out of it. God forbid, it might just make me a little more mindful in the process. The choice faced by every person is simple. The path social media users are taking, one of scary others, has but one violent end—at best, civil unrest and homegrown terror attacks, at worst, full-on civil war. I have neither the appetite nor the energy for anything short of comprehensive social media regulation.

I propose we find a new western priority, shaped by balance and coexistence, by spaces where bridges are built across time, over species, and between each other. Otherwise, social media behavior becomes invasive in a fragile democracy, pushing out the native fauna of individuality and compassion. In its wake is a bloated, overfed frog in the shallows of a collective psyche.

We need biodiversity of thought and biodiversity in our communities. Together, users could bring down this rapacious beast with full hearts and radical kindness.

My paternal grandparents lived in the house next to my parents. Spread between them was a fenceless plot laid beneath birch trees, drooping willows, and crowded pines. A tall apple tree grew nearest to our house with wooden planks nailed into the trunk. One morning, during an unseasonably cool summer, my siblings devised a plan to build a treehouse in its sturdy boughs. Other things intervened, the cost of supplies exceeded our limits, and the project was abandoned. Before they knew it, school started and homework took priority.

My father's sheep grazed beneath apple blossoms, roaming plots of grass and a small orchard of peaches. By the time I was a teenager, the sheep were replaced by rows of plants where corn, squash, peppers, and tomatoes emerged from freshly tilled earth. When dinner approached, my mother ushered us into the kitchen, carrying fresh vegetables in ten-pound flour sacks.

Cooking was typically reserved for women in rural Mormon households while men worked in coal mines and power plants. Forgoing tradition, my mom welcomed me with my sisters in the kitchen. We started with recipes she learned as a child: breads, stir-fries, soups, fruit pies, and, of course, green Jell-O and funeral potatoes—an aptly named casserole dish often served during Mormon funerals. Much of what we cooked was inspired by post-Depression foods my mother ate as a child, making extensive use of flours, fats, and salts. We explored how these ingredients could be improved each Saturday morning when cooking shows aired on public television. My eldest sister sat closest to the screen, ready to pop up and adjust the rabbit ears when programs faded to static. On its surface, my childhood was pleasant, nurturing, and loving, but only from the outside looking in.

—

By eight p.m., Ferron has gone dark. We drive to a church lot and wait, parked near an old white dumpster illuminated by nearby lampposts. Outside the vehicle, leguminous seed pods rattle as they blow over the pavement. My father is angry. His fists are balled against the steering wheel. He decides to take this out on me. "If you took care of your appearance," he says, "maybe people would want to be seen with you." He reaches over and pinches long curls of my hair between his fingers. "You really need a haircut. People will think you're a queer."

My hair had grown to my shoulders. Salons were for sissies, I thought. I was always fighting this inner turmoil of how my thoughts manifested in external appearances. I once tried shaving my head to conceal my sexuality. I wore camouflage and trucker hats to further this heterosexual transformation. I tried many things to make my image match my faith, to make him happy, to feel welcome in my home and community. Even after reconstructing my appearance into a farmer toughing it out in the wilderness, I failed to recognize myself. For me, camouflage was more than attire, it was a state of being, a knowing that I was inherently, fundamentally different from my surroundings. It was in that cover that I gained the trust and affection of those around me, but it was fragile. If they saw me, truly saw me, they would know I didn't belong.

His angry mutterings turn toward my mother. "This is why you don't get married. She's trailer trash. Women are good-for-nothing wastes of human flesh. How I'd love to cave her face in . . ." He trails off, slamming his fists against the dashboard.

My mother was a hoarder, gathering clothes and knick-knacks to fill emotional voids carved by poverty, her own complicated relationship with her father, and now by an insolent husband. Her condition worsened. Piles of personal effects occupied much of the house, divided by narrow paths to walk from room to room. My bedroom was soon consumed by mounds of her attire, forcing me to migrate to the living room couch, which was threadbare and polished with sweat. In these accumulations, trusted community members saw an ungovernable housewife, but I saw something else. I saw traumas softened by material goods, voids shaped by the absence of love and belonging.

Her actions caused us great difficulty, especially when she refused my assistance. I woke each morning to cabinets that drooped from moldy walls, groaning when items were pulled from shelves. Rusty knives were jammed in the drains to keep them flowing. None of the dishes had been properly washed for years, so I bought my own and concealed them in a dresser where they wouldn't provoke an argument over sanitation. The fridge, thirty years old and puttering, was chock-full of expired food to be served and eaten. Everything else was soaked in improperly stored raw meat juices. Mice and bugs roamed through the house, squealing each night from nocturnal raids adjacent to where I slept, or tried to. I stayed up late, slept little, and woke paralyzed. I was told this was normal, that trauma was never the same for everyone, and mine just so happened to involve palpitations, sleep paralysis, and moments where hours passed in the span of minutes. But I was also deeply sympathetic. I grew up watching her brightness dim as she looked in mirrors, puffing her cheeks, swiveling her torso in revulsion. She saw in herself a fictional being: overweight, unwanted, unsightly. No matter how she malnourished her body or indulged in harmful shopping behaviors, she saw the person she was trained to see.

"Have you tried being nicer to her? Helping around the house?" I asked my father.

"You want me to kill myself?" he replied, his forehead veins ballooning. "That's what I'm going to do! Let that hang on your head. I bet your mother killed herself because of you. That's what you do. You cause everyone problems." He stepped out and slammed the door, leaving the truck shaking.

His words brought me back to their argument. My father had planned an intervention with her family, something to "fix" her, to demonstrate that she—without any provocation from him—was the source of all problems. To my mother, it seemed like a blank check for his behavior, leveraging her further from external support. Shortly thereafter, she jumped in a vehicle and fled down the highway. In my childish imaginings, I was afraid that she had taken her life. What more could she lose? I thought it was somehow my fault. If only I was less gay, less awkward, and more capable.

He and my mother fought every day into the early hours of morning, always looming above my makeshift bed, more concerned about winning, about gaining an upper hand. Inevitably, his arguments turned toward assigning blame for failing to change my "ways." They were so consumed in their quarrels they both forgot to do much. Doctor appointments went unscheduled. Dentist visits were out of the question. Mandatory immunizations went ignored. Injuries healed in all the wrong ways. I saw through a haze school blackboards and Gaussian-blurred canyons. Perhaps this defined my compulsion for color, an absence of sight where one discovers only shade, intensity, and structure. Vivid, membranous beauty. I lived in this milky snow globe of lucent color for ten years until I acquired glasses and witnessed the desert in a new, daunting clarity.

In all of this, I felt something entirely different: reliance. I had divorced myself from humanity. My survival depended upon that. Yet, I was human and I needed them, especially when they weren't there. On my own, I had to learn everything from watching others: how to wash clothes, tie my shoes, my feeble attempt at riding a bike. For lessons on life, I followed the guidance of wild animals, binoculars in hand, learning how to navigate humanity encroaching on us both.

I felt the burn of my parents' absence in my nostrils, floating through pools of the Great Basin Desert, their viridian depths teaching that one must sink or swim. Locals came to warn me away, reciting stories of poor swimmers knocking their heads against inner volcanic protrusions. This was no way to learn, they said, motioning to skeletons imagined lying somewhere in the abyss. I slid in anyway, feeling the jet of geothermal water stretch between my toes, unexpected heat rising over my chest. I inhaled and dropped beneath the surface, slivers of light slipping past my eyes.

—

The river is frozen. We navigate with our toes curled, gripping the ice. I slip and tumble into a rock; its sharp, needlelike point punctures me between vertebra and pelvis. I can't walk. Tingling fizzes through my conscious, down my spine. Everything hurts. Bulbs of white light flash through my side-vision. I hobble-crawl to the truck and we drive home. Doctors are for other children.

—

I write to reconcile traumas. It is a task neither easy nor clear-cut. It is an overgrown trail of emotions. I see my parents grow older, make progress. Or maybe I become more distanced from their behavior. Nonetheless, I still love them. Though, love does not erase trauma, it covers it, and truth is buried by the ever-changing complexities of our relationship. It is easy to hate a person, to exist on two islands separated by cruelty and nothing but cruelty. Loving is harder. Having parents who are deeply dysfunctional but somehow still loving is a thing most difficult to resolve. It burdens me with navigating a roadmap between love and suffering, but those feelings become woefully indistinguishable, a single circle on a Venn diagram. I end up between them, feeling somehow culpable for my lack of guidance. I feel guilty for feeling bad.

The erosion of my childhood created a habitat most nourishing for wild spaces. Plants inevitably took root in the sediments of my grief, sprouting silvery leaves uniquely adapted to thrive in harsh environments. These immature leaves are lined with the finest of hairs known as trichomes. Trichomes can protect the plant from various detriments like excess sunlight, evaporative water loss, or pesky insects waiting to chow down on its vegetative bits. They are also wise teachers, reminding me that I can't always change my environment, but sometimes, when the opportunity presents itself, I can adapt to them. I can heal, nourish others, and find community in the soils I am given. These are the promises of a desert. It is an offering of healing ingredients. But what is mine and my responsibility is the recipe, the special arrangement of hope and longing.

When I think of the Sonoran Desert, I often think of Robert Villa. With dark, curly hair and brown eyes that widen with fascination, Robert has an intense, warm energy, much like the landscapes he so cherishes.

It was no surprise to see that his vehicle was also sculpted by his arid presence, filled with cobblestones, bleached white bones, and skeletons of old, withered branches—twisted and crackled beneath his gray fabric seats.

Perfumed by the intoxicating scent of sage, we rode up Tumamoc Hill, a nature reserve west of Tucson operated by the University of Arizona. (*Tumamoc* translates to "regal horned lizard" in the Tohono O'odham language—a flattened, wide-bodied reptile known scientifically as *Phrynosoma solare*, native to the American Southwest and Mexico.) Near the top, with the city sprawled in the distance, Robert opened the door to a greenhouse and welcomed me inside.

Robert is a naturalist of a rare caliber, residing at the mental confluence of art and science. Often with a violin in tow, he feels compelled to serenade ancient carvings, or plants beginning to bud. Accompanying him often reminds me of a scene from the 1988 Japanese animated fantasy *My Neighbor Totoro*, where two young girls learn from the forest spirit that ritual dance can give rise to newborn oak trees. Writer Jessica Cockerill describes the film as "ecological magic," which is an equally fitting description of Robert.

At the Desert Laboratory on Tumamoc Hill, Robert cares for flora both familiar and obscure, many inhabiting the remote areas south of the US-Mexico border. Inside the facility, bewitching milkvines drape from the ceiling, rejoicing in a pocket of humidity. Other rare or unusual species reach outward from pots lined against the walls, including stunning, steely leaved succulents. I ask him which is his favorite. Like a good caretaker, he chooses to avoid the question.

He takes me outside where rocks are stacked in piles, tracing the constructions of the Hohokam, an archaeological culture spanning the first century AD to about AD 1450. The name, Hohokam, is an Akimel O'odham word translating to "all used up." As is often the case, this is a term prescribed by archaeologists, referring to agricultural populations in southern Arizona. Some present-day tribal members have proposed much broader, more encompassing names, like the "Ancestral Sonoran Desert Peoples."

The mounds, Robert recalls, mitigate water loss and rodent predation to support the growing of agaves. These plants were cultivated by the Hohokam people as an important source of food, especially in months where other crops or wild plants were unreliable or otherwise unproductive. The genus, *Agave*, comprises about forty species, some of which are still widely used today in brewing tequila and the smoky beverage mezcal, made from oven-cooked agaves and distilled primarily in the Mexican state of Oaxaca.

As we part from the garden and head back toward the vehicle, our conversation shifts to the places that hold our hearts. Robert grins as he reminisces over the Colorado River's estuary in Mexico.

His place, the Colorado River Delta, is fed by waters flowing through redrock canyons of Utah and Arizona, as the Colorado River pummels the region's deep crimson walls into submission. The memory of sandstone cliffs, reduced to individual grains, flows southward to the sea. Where they meet is a counterbalance of oceans: one of water, the other of sand.

The delta is now frequented by the Colorado River's sun-baked apparition—a dry, vanishing watercourse, a consequence of upstream dams and irrigation. Among them, the Glen Canyon Dam destroyed not only hundreds of miles of downstream ecosystems, but wondrous, mystic canyons flooded by the rising waters in Lake Powell. When I visited the area with Aaron and his mother, you could almost feel seven hundred feet of concrete grinding in your teeth, holding back everything but a monkey wrench. A truly ironic sign in front reads: *Defacing our natural features destroys our heritage. Vandalism is unsightly and illegal.*

My late pal Katie Lee was a fierce opponent to the dam and a lover of sensuous desert water. I met her while working on my first book, an anthology of our love and loss of sacred places. Over the years, we exchanged photos, memories, and bittersweet stories. She talked of her ghost river—how she bathed as madly in light as in water, how she found artifacts and sensed in them ancient hands, how she held them to the sun like cosmic gifts before placing them back to their devoted bearers. When I asked if she wanted to return, she replied: *Well, sweetie: [I've] been there, done that, and am so very glad I have! Are we blessed? Yes!* Then a resident of Tucson, she, like me, flowed south, trailing the thin blue line of the Colorado River.

I thought of the Colorado River as it traveled through my home place, sliced between two loaves of burgundy Kayenta sandstone. As a child, I walked its fertile edges, looking over its waters the color of muddy green Jurassic chert to observe kayakers docked on its opposite bank, nearly eclipsed in mirage. On summer days I scuffled through tamarisk forests, nearly poking out an eyeball or two—all to witness great blue herons poised in foliate shallows, legs raised in suspended yoga poses. Once school attendance precluded these visits, I waited in the parking lot of the Ferron Mercantile off Main Street, looking to their pale baby-blue feathers and muddy white and black bellies flying overhead. Their shade, an iceberg blue, paired so well with the cerulean sky. With the eyes of a kindergartener, I saw them as primordial beasts. The word *pterodactyl* fell from my lips more than a few times. I wondered if they were lost teratorns—large avian scavengers that went extinct some ten thousand years ago with terrifying wing spans reaching ten to twenty feet. Now with whatever wisdom I have gleaned, I see them as a signal of the future, flying a path I would one day travel with my beloved to a new home.

Are we blessed?

Yes!

January 1, 2010

Confusion.

I feel a lot of that lately. I feel crazy for wishing things were simpler, because simpler usually means *worse*. Last night, I was reading coming out stories and, if I'm being honest with myself, I felt envious. I understand that coming out is a difficult thing and there is significant privilege in having a home and a family in its aftermath. But I still need resolution, even if I lose everything in my wanting. Is that too much to ask? Mormonism, at least my community's brand of it, isn't straightforward. Difficult thoughts are repressed. Emotions are hidden. If there was any resentment, it would be reserved for local gossip, never spoken to my face. It feels like I'm experiencing my relationships from the other side of a peephole. Blurry figures, muffled words. They can be so nice to me, and so cruel. Kindness is delivered with forked tongues. When is a compliment withering condemnation? When is kindness manipulation? When is acceptance just a ploy of superiority?

Whispers, chatter, gossip.

Recently, I received text messages from a member of my family. They intended them for somebody else. Within them, they claim that I am not a smart person, that gay people are an abomination, that they feel sorrow watching a person fall so far from the faithful wagon. What hurts most is their patronizing grief, their sadness that weeps from a wound of self-admiration.

I cannot forgive of what I am not aware.

Honesty. Even if it breaks relationships or becomes something that pains me more, confusion can be worse than rejection because loving and hurting blurs boundaries. I hate that I still can't trust people, not even my family. I hate that every genuine compliment is delivered like a knife to my chest.

I just don't know.

I don't know.

I never know.

Juniper Roots

Who is the president?
Where are you?
. . . your name?

Her name is Lisa, I think. A light in her hands is pointed into an eye she has just pried open. The world is white, but I am somewhere else. Sound is muffled, her voice sizzling behind a dull, planetary hum. Has that noise always been there? I think just a few minutes have passed but it feels like hours since I last felt my body. Wherever I may be, time runs like a slurry of clay paste. I feel silly. I have experienced such sadness, so much anxiety, unbearable grief. I have tried to keep a watchful eye for a disaster that never comes. Yet it all leads to this, and I am dead.

In the white plane, there is nothing. No beam of light, no darkness, no angels or deities, no pearly gates to await life's judgment. I am a blank screen on a monitor that has dropped to the floor. I am empty and infinite. My family, I worry for them. My mother has lost so many people: her father, three sisters, her beloved grandmother Burnice. How could she also lose her son? She is a warm, anxious woman with curly, eighties-style blond hair. She once bought me a glittery pink ring when I was a child, knowing my father would disapprove, knowing it was confirmation of my "feminine inclinations." It was a small act of acceptance and I loved her for it.

I relate to my body by a single umbilical cord. Its scent is musk-like, fragrant, filled with nostalgia of canyon mesas. Junipers! As minutes translate to hours, I feel myself privy to this juniper world. I sense the exchange of carbon dioxide to oxygen—nature's pulmonary vein supplying the atmosphere with fresh, breathable air. I think of anatomy and how, if our forests are truly the lungs of the planet, they are also the canaries in our coal mines, how I had seen them skeletonized by juniper bark beetles and downwind radiation, the effects of climate change and gluttonous desire. I feel their presence as an interconnected network of trees, roots gnarled and twined over miles. Their wooden trails were mine to explore as an airy wanderer until I felt its pain, or my own. There is no telling.

I think of rock falls: canyon floors marked with scars—sharp edges, unsettling white sandstone stripped naked of its iron and manganese oxides. Provocative geologic pornography. I think of being struck by hundreds of pounds of tumbling rock: how its momentum felt in my abdomen; how it sent me backwards with the brute force of an eighteen-wheeler; how far I fell down this scimitar of ivory sandstone. My body facedown on the ground. Dead.

With nostrils full of juniper sap, I regain the sensation of my body, but this takes its time. Vision comes to me slowest of all. And when it returns, I see things I wish I hadn't: blood covers my shorts and calves, muscle exposed through my thigh. Above me, search and rescue works quickly, rigging a stretcher to a tree that survived the rock collapse. I hear my father's voice muttering from behind, urging me to get a blessing. Faith over life.

This was his hope: that I would find Mormonism after this death—accidental as it may be—or on the edge of it, and return. I always feared that if I died, my family would censor my story. Knowing my preference for cremation, they would hoist me into the earth. Hymns would follow, a ceremony to close the book I had sacrificed everything to pry open. They would say I was a devout follower of the Church of Jesus Christ of Latter-day Saints, that my testimony was as rigid as my spirit. Then, nothing—I would be another faithful limb on this colorless family tree. Even on the outside of faith, I was less of a person than a follower. I could not be a disbeliever but was *inactive.* I could revoke my baptism, declare my opposition to the faith, and they would still try to send a child to be baptized in my place.

I wonder if I am alone in this nebulous pedigree, or if others had vanished to the heavy hand of family desire. Even if I lose my life, I want my identity in its wake.

—

After severe physical trauma, the room didn't stop spinning for weeks. None of the medications seemed to do anything. I found a word for this: "agony," derived from the Greek word *agōnia*, in reference to the struggle to win an athletic competition, and eventually adopted to describe the pain that followed. There was something less noble in being on a stretcher while nurses sanitized my muscle with bristle brushes, scrubbing out the rocks lodged deep inside my leg.

"Just a little longer," they reassured me. "Your surgeon just finished up his cattle appointments. His last was an unruly heifer."

I noted minutes by the pop of needle punctures, suturing me back together. And the pain, even long after, coursed over my body in currents of nausea, dizziness, throbbing; followed by head pressure, high-pitched ringing, and a sudden loss of consciousness. Wake up, repeat. I wanted out. Out! My body was bruised a deep purple, my foot several sizes too swollen, my leg sunken inward where the outlines of muscle used to be, and there were some below-the-belt areas that shouldn't have been bleeding, or so I've been told, but I still ripped out the IV, burst through the hospital doors, and shimmied on my knees to the nearest unnamed feature on the topo map—if only in my imagination.

Thus was life for several months, bedridden and far from capable of roaming the desert, though crutches soon opened the possibility of nefarious, doctor-unapproved walkabouts.

"Remember, Jonathan, not to swim with dead animal fluids for at least a few months," he warned, squinting his eyes in reluctant concession. "This medication is especially not suitable for your tendency toward swamps."

I was picked up by Connie Massingale, my hiking compadre who had recently undergone a total knee replacement. Both of us were escapees running from the tyranny of rest and recuperation, afflicted with a bad case of wanderlust. Hours passed, so too did rabbits, sage, a shaggy bunch of pronghorn, fifteen pull-tab beer cans placed on fence posts. We parked and walked through a canyon, passing cottonwoods and cryptic figures pecked in tight alcoves. The leaves nestled beneath our feet, contributing to the earthy smells of winter, wind stabbing at our fingertips, our feet plunged happily in technically-not-swamps. She waited up ahead while I dragged my crutches over the river cobble, pausing frequently to put on—or take off—clothes. This season in canyon country was notorious for its wild fluctuations in temperature.

What the fuck are you doing?

The thought caught me by surprise. I struggled to repress it.

You do not matter.

There are precious few moments when we see the brittle of life. This was mine. I felt my body changing like seasons, where one thing shifts to another. I felt these things: kinship, fear, uncertainty of where my life was headed. But I was also happy—happy to be with her and to be here, to watch dried leaves swirl through canyon pools in inky blots. I thought I would be okay, but I doubted this knowing. I cried quietly, feeling like the world was turning and I was not. I feared my pain would last forever, that my physical injuries would never heal, as they were as open and bleeding as my heart.

I coiled my fingers around my leg, noticing blood draining through the gauze. It felt like hell. I clenched it tighter. It burned like a manifestation of my self-doubt.

I think we should go home now.

Do they even remember what they've done to you? The thought spins in my head like an engine that won't turn over, thinking of church, of school, of family. I see their faces in newspapers accompanied with words I try to accept. Honor. Dignity. Respect. Words they have not earned but taken. They must know they belong to someone else. But then I feel other things, like guilt, because this thinking resembles revenge.

Journal Entry: September 3, 2020

I bear a scar of juniper roots. Seven years later and my sensation never fully returned, but I feel you in my presence, Old Juniper. I can trail my fingers along my skin, feeling the polished, disfigured flesh as finely as I feel your weathered branches. I feel you—only you. The Navajo word for "juniper" is *gad*. As Ellen Meloy notes, you are but one letter from being divined a deity, yet I find this syllable all the more powerful. You are used in ceremony and medicine, in simmering blue corn mush and scrolls of paper-thin piki bread. I feel you on my lips, in my heart, and on my skin. I am grateful for everything you have given me, be it life, or a glimpse beyond its fragile boughs.

Daydreaming

I'm not sure when things started changing. At home, I hear my father next to the fireplace, Fender in hand, singing the lines to "Muskrat Love" with the squeak of his acoustic guitar sliding as he adjusts notes. It is a happy place. I cuddle next to my sister beneath blankets while we wait for the chorus to swim into the airwaves, daydreaming about our place in the cosmos. Outside, the snow is falling like a Christmas card cliché, and our giant rosebush keeps pockets of snow tight against the windowsills. My father leans the guitar against his chair as he exits the basement, gathering wood and coal to keep us warm in this spool of smoke.

Sometimes, when the weather hit hard, our power vanished for hours, sometimes days. When this happened, my mom entered the basement with her arms full of ingredients from Ferron Mercantile. Often, these ingredients were accompanied by canned vegetables from last season's harvest. Logs were put in the fireplace to get it screaming hot, followed by an orchestra of cooking, cracking, and stirring above the flames.

I always admired her tenacity. She was tough and indomitable. Her parents were the products of the Great Depression, as were my father's, and they learned to persist through the worst: war, hunger, drought. In rural Utah, far away from any semblance of assistance, people became fiercely self-reliant and severely impoverished. My grandfather was known to subsist on bread and whole cream with a light pinch of sugar. Though the Depression was over by the time my mother came to being, many families were still uncomfortable embracing worldly comforts, partly for tradition, but mostly because self-sustainment reliably kept their heads above water. From the age of twelve, my mom was already baking six loaves of bread per day, with hungry brothers waiting at the table. It was a persistence of spirit that didn't take time to cope with her younger sister's death, or the trauma of cradling her lifeless body because she felt love demanded it.

Beyond the confines of our cozy abode, temperatures ticked downward come winter. Negative ten. Negative twenty. At one point, the thermometer on our shed dipped to sixty degrees below freezing. That night we lost our Douglas firs to a fog that buried town, exposed only at their trunks with glints of gray-green pigment tilted skyward. We listened to the Tabernacle Choir—the church's dedicated hymn group—whose ethereal vocals transformed into a haunting foretell of the end of this world as "Abide with Me" carved into the silence.

Music was always important to me. Some music changed with the seasons. This was not a deliberate tradition; there were simply some songs that resonated with the nestle of winter. On summer nights, classical music burned through the crackle of bad speakers, and this was allegedly one of my first and fleeting childhood obsessions. As I got older, I found more in common with the zing of Elton John, who, despite being gay, was reluctantly permitted to fill our household with his "Crocodile Rock." I suspect his talent for weaving a contagious earworm had something to do with evading censorship. Besides, we rarely listened to the words. At least, not until they started cutting deep:

"If you only knew
What I'm going through
Time and again I get ashamed
To say your name"

Music opened the door to communities beyond my own. As I entered my teenage years, this door opened wide with the rise of Lady Gaga. This was the era of the common American grappling with the idea of homosexuality, only a handful of years after a person could be arrested if caught "being gay," although it was rarely prosecuted. Most commonly, LGBTQ+ people were relegated to bad humor on family sitcoms—the "effeminizing men is the only joke in our playbook" era of television—or hinted at in eccentric villains. Gaga forced visibility with unconventional fashion choices, which escaped censorship both in media and within family homes. The genius was that her message was never explicit, but many LGBTQ+ people watching her perform "Bad Romance" on television saw safe spaces beyond the horizons of our knowing.

—

Summer fulfilled the yin-yang cycle of Ferron's weather, from punishing cold to sticky heat. When the temperature became unbearable, we wandered up into the mountains in a small truck that could hardly accommodate five energetic children. We typically stayed in the evergreen forests for a few days, exploring the insects and wildflowers that sought their livelihood in crisp mountain springs. With my trusty wand-stick to cast away the Boy Scouts, we wandered into the unknowable, ripe with possibility. I encountered slimy black salamanders and freshwater shrimp, old plane wrecks and hidden pools. On occasion, we witnessed cult activity and mystic symbols. It was a place of its own conscious being, where sunlight scarcely penetrated the canopy, where you lose yourself to your whims and listen to the trees breathing. For hours. Weeks. It was easy to get lost. When I was a boy, an adopted schoolkid attempted to cross in the middle of winter. He froze to death trying to find his birth home. I knew what it was like to be afraid of new homes. We had outside discussions and inside discussions. Cloak-and-dagger dialogues kept Child Protective Services from knowing about the abuses. The threat of being taken away kept me quiet. The threat of dying in a snowbank made me obey.

—

I remember when the membrane of my world ruptured.

"What will we do about Mom's anorexia?"

I was up in the mountains, but these words felt like drowning. I knew, then, that my childhood was over. I don't know whether these words spoke of things beyond my childish knowing, or if speaking manifested them into being, but life nevertheless took a new trajectory.

We came home to the faint smell of vomit on her clothing and a house in disarray. My mom was frantic, saying that she had people following her, abusing her, groping her. She proceeded to cover the television and computer screens with blankets so "they" couldn't watch her. Vehicles in different styles and colors crossed the street, each somehow specific to her stalkers, the government, or another group from her internal map of paranoia. This was when the hoarding started, and when outside people were banned from the inside.

She began losing weight, a lot of it, and her teeth eroded from her face. She replaced them with layers of superglue affixed to her gums and largely stopped eating altogether. Trusted leaders from our local church told us that it was "natural for a woman to want to be skinny," and encouraged us to keep her that way.

My father's anger burned redder. Household items were broken against the floor. Screaming replaced the gentle strum of his guitar. I wondered if the cracks in her spirit had spread to him, or if this was an overpouring of behind-the-door behavior from my father. I didn't know what to believe, which path to take toward normalcy. One evening I saw his fist balled close to her face and I fled from the house, running until my feet throbbed. I felt blameworthy for my cowardice, for being a bad mediator. I knew when his energy entered chaos, when it was easy to come into his scrutiny. I wanted nothing to do with it. No one was spared of his outbursts, not even our pets, who he threatened to murder on many occasions with a firearm clutched in his fingers. It was instinct that made me run, a panic that flashed through my limbs until I made it anywhere but home.

I kept running, sensing the pavement shift to gravel beneath my feet, to a place where wild birds gathered: blue jays, red-winged blackbirds, the occasional turkey vulture on a thermal path invisible to my plane of seeing. I kept running until it hurt, because I hurt, and the sting in my lungs made me feel something I could conceptualize.

Mussentuchit Badlands

When I was a child, I searched for bones, scouring hillsides for orbs of white so distinct and revealing. Today the raven is one of my treasures, a few feathers tasseling from his taut beak, segments of wing remaining, outstretched as if to feel the source of thermals he once so proudly maneuvered. His body, more barren than the rest, looks like an assortment of goodies he would collect if given the opportunity. He snapped through the park's garbage a month earlier, after which he lined his merchandise on a bench, prioritizing only the best to carry home. His bones are now jumbled with bits of windblown ribbon and tin. An irony I hope he would have appreciated.

I cherished bones as they had a topography of their own, bleached white, gritty to the touch like sandpaper, shaped into basins and gorges by the ebb and flow of osseous matter. Of special salience were the sutures, structures that allow the skulls of youngins to grow and develop, flowing unimpeded like tiny rivers you could raft beneath the tips of your fingers. It was an early lesson in scale, as I found landscapes that could vanish under the cover of my thumb.

As charming as the bones may be, I never took my discoveries home. They were not mine to take. They belonged to the wind as it swept through the long valleys of piñon. They belonged to decomposition and the earth. They belonged to many things, but they did not belong to me.

—

When I hiked into the deserts, I experienced the flesh and blood of wilderness, but not its bones. Everything was layered with soil and vegetative matter, or covered with almost too much rock. Even prominent canyons of the San Rafael Swell consisted of deep green rivers of ponderosa and sage. I cherished these spaces, of course, but I was also disappointed. There must be something beneath, something I was missing, an omission to the visible desert.

And then I found the Mussentuchit Badlands.

As its name suggests, the Mussentuchit Badlands hides a deeper understanding. A knowing you simply "mustn't touch."* But I also wasn't one for following rules.

These badlands border on the indescribable, more apocalyptic than you might expect, soaked with blood-red clays and volcanic intrusions, tattered beneath igneous rock, rounded and polished like oversized cannonballs. In some cases, sandstone is heaved upwards by two-story-high walls of grayish volcanic intrusions. Giant fins dissect much of the region, some no wider than a kitchen tile but spread outward for hundreds of feet. These features are known as volcanic dikes, formed when ancient magma settled in cracks and crevices, solidified, and emerged when the softer surrounding rocks eroded, leaving thin fins of rock reminiscent of semi-submerged sea monsters.

The longer I spent in the badlands, the more I learned about the desert. Despite its desolate appearance, plants still eke out a living, surviving drifting sands through deep underground rhizomes—features that can produce the shoots and root systems of new plants, also storing nutrients like starch and proteins, allowing them to propagate and survive in such unfavorable conditions. Other species, like *Parthenium ligulatum*, Colorado

---

* The origin of the name has a few different stories, with most citing the alkaline-rich and toxic waters. Others cite the abundance of plants in the genus Astragalus, which are toxic to livestock.

feverfew, survive by staying close to the ground on wind-eroded surfaces, occupying mats speckled with white flowers not much larger than a pen tip. In these spaces, I remembered that survival sometimes depended on sheltering down, spreading outward, surviving through the desert like rhizome shoots.

—

The Mussentuchit Badlands is a hard-won space, one without showy canyons of redrock that attract people by the thousands. But those majestic symbols of the West provide just one way of knowing the desert. Solitude is another. So, when development came knocking at the badlands' door, I pushed back, much to the chagrin of some conservationists, who felt the badlands should be sacrificed to oil and gas in the service of future proposals preserving other lands.

Aaron and I spent weeks backpacking through the region in protest, slithering through slot canyons and open plains, towing notebooks and gear to testify to its vast emptiness. We discovered that, much like the raven's bones, its bareness was superficial, nested within landscapes of rib and vertebra, perhaps a hint of its beating heart. In its blazoned chest were carpets of agate, hypnotically saturated hillsides, blackened marbles propped on the whitest of pedestals, and sandscapes that poured against deep crimson spires, worn smooth like sand castles. Near to these features, in a seldom-visited corner of Capitol Reef National Park, are the names of places of heart-aching poetry: Temple of the Sun, Temple of the Moon, and Glass Mountain—a dome of glittering earth, a frontispiece like two Gothic temples looming hundreds of feet skyward. Beyond, the cliffs are blood-red, joined by arroyo arteries and a liver of buff-red Entrada Sandstone that detoxifies even the most stubborn spirits.

We saw truth beneath the flesh. We compiled documents of our data and argued for the region's archaeological, biological, geological, and paleontological treasures, in addition to essential and endangered resources like silence and solitude. Little to our surprise, a new species of tyrannosaur, *Moros intrepidus*, the "harbinger of doom," was found in the Mussentuchit Badlands just a few years later. The discovery of *M. intrepidus* suggests an earlier invasion of smaller three-to-four-foot tyrannosaurs from Asia to the US, preceding the iconic *Tyrannosaurus rex* by about thirty million years. This wayfaring, "intrepid" dinosaur earns its name from these travels, eventually settling in a landscape of rivers, lakes, and floodplains that would become the Mussentuchit Badlands desert as known today.

We presented our findings to the Bureau of Land Management and argued that the area should be spared from extraction. The BLM heard our pleas and the leases were deferred—at least, for the time being. Without formal protections, they can come back in a few years, in five, in a decade—who knows? But like the fragile bodies of wandering desert creatures, wilderness is reliant on a framework of protection. I need the plants, the animals, the alluring redrock canyons—but I also need the bones: spaces of sere nothingness where so few raise their voice in support.

A Personal Topography of Hue and Color

As a young boy, I professed yellow to be my favorite color. I loved sunflowers and autumnal light, and the thin, bundled stalks of prince's plume that flowered in April. But mostly, I loved it because my classmates did not. They saw yellow as defilement and an utter lack of grace, the color of swamp water and rotting sink sponges. In the desert, yellow is the color of transience, persuading easily to red or blue. If I loved it too intensely, it felt like it could vanish forever, slip from our hands like sunlight or a stiff breeze. Students, I thought, feared this impermanence and returned home with cinched coats and crossed arms, holding tight to a color not unlike our youth.

My passion for yellow grew over years and miles—an affinity cemented when I traveled to blocks of yellow ochre. They were tucked beneath painted quail with fat bellies and handsome topknots. The lowest of the couplings waddled at ground level to bulbous cliffs in scarlet. In their centers were sunny orbs that gave color to their central feathers. Their beauty was ancient, a thousand years old, yet preserved as if coated in a timeless lacquer.

I loved yellow, truly and dearly, until I didn't. I had a yellow-enamored teacher, one with a predisposition for making students choose heterosexual brides in magazines. One day she wore all yellow, pulled up a chair, and began reading a story.

The tale described a boy—a young, eager kid who got into an accident and needed a blood transfusion. She described a mishap: the transfusion had given him a sexually transmitted disease. "It is ironic," she said, "that this was how he ended up with the disease, as he was gay, and we know how they sleep around." Then, after a long, gut-wrenching decision, yellow lost a bit of its light, and purple, the color of rarity and royalty, was a choice free of her contamination.

In the desert, purple is the color of absence. It does not exist but in scant quantities, in corner-of-the-eye observations. You may find it on igneous boulders, on blanks of patina so stained and weathered that indigo traces its edges. It is fugitive color, invisible in most light, and unstable when seen. Ghostly apparitions exhibit it, painted on cliffs and alcove ceilings, though conceived in blood-red concoctions. After thousands of years and exposure to atmospheric oxygen, their hue shifted to silvery magenta, a shade that reflects sunlight like ghost-shaped mirrors.

Purple was the color I took to my high school principal when Jack Denton Reese, a seventeen-year-old gay Utahn, killed himself. It was my hope that wearing it shamelessly would make us visible. I sat in a meeting, surrounded by a half-dozen middle-aged men, and testified to my experiences. I attested to the value of suicidal students. I asked them to participate in Spirit Day, the third Thursday in October, by wearing purple in solidarity against LGBTQ+ bullying. The proposal was rejected on all counts, without pause or deliberation.

Of all colors, I disliked red the most. It was the color of anger and zealousness, brute force, and unjustified power. In my child mind, it was a color befitting of my father, who had adopted it as his favorite. Through my youth, I spent hours concealing any items that could be categorized as red. Rosy-cheeked dolls were among my victims, who I turned to face the wall in shame. Crimson shirts were stuffed into dresser drawers, never to be seen again. I was one permanent marker away from scribbling the word from every book, just as my father had done with unforgivable curses like damn and hell.

Despite cliffs, and pigment, and carmine-helmeted woodpeckers, red was a tough sell. I sidestepped any cognitive dissonance by seeing redrock as kind-of-orange and pictographs as almost-barely-brown. It took years and long contemplative sojourns until I accepted the color completely. It was only in the realization that red is the color of inner conflict—a reflection of anger or passion, affection or violence—that I learned to understand it with more compassion. It is a color like my father, whose love was eclipsed by doctrine and mental illness. It is a color of irreconcilable actions, but also sadness. You look back toward a distressed child who subsisted on parasitic emotions: greed, animosity, arrogance. Overt redness. You feel heartbroken for that person, but deep down, you wonder if there's anything left of the host, the inner child. You only see their remaining color, a red like bloodstained hands.

The red of a desert is that color reconciled. All other colors rely upon it to carry water, to capture pollen, and to provide vegetative nutrients. It is in the dissonances of red, its potential for neutrality, that these wild balances are sustained. Among its tortuous, unyielding, yet surprisingly delicate topographies, there is no err in a distinctively red Colorado Plateau.

Red is balanced by turquoise—a color carried around necks hundreds of years ago, on warm, sweat-beaded skin. It was transported far to the south, to Aztecs and Mayans, where it inlaid lifelike masks and double-headed serpents. In exchange, denizens of the Colorado Plateau obtained macaws, copper bells, and prized cacao.

Turquoise is the color of my eyes, its blueness borne by neither parent. It is the color of distance, and faith. Perhaps it is also the color of loss. I stood on the foothills of the Wasatch Mountains, looking onward to the Salt Lake City temple. On the horizon, it appeared as an atmospheric blue, vanishing as the gap between us deepened. There came a time when I could no longer see it, a point on the skyline, a memory of where something once stood.

Hiking with my friend Diane Orr is like seeing with impressionistic eyes. I would often find her holed up behind the rocks, dusted in a cocktail of clay powder and mouse droppings. What may seem to most as dark and unsanitary revealed to her the inner workings of sunlight and shadow. This was no surprise. Diane is also a photographer. For many years she hauled a metal box known as the Hulcherama through the canyons. The Hulcher, as she called it, was a shutterless camera capable of producing 360-degree images on film, giving Diane the opportunity to explore rock art images and their landscapes in a seamless composition. With it she reveals a deep knowing of the desert, from prairies to small cavities, juxtaposing containment with openness. We became friends in no small part due to our love of these dark places—underworlds. Exploring caves, alcoves, and the cavities beneath rocks was like reading confessionals written in dark, concentrated ink.

Many years after meeting Diane, I suggested a visit to a canyon well-suited to her love of these spaces. We packed our cameras, camping gear, and a bed for her slobber-hound, Luna, and left for the great kind-of-unknown. A few hours into the drive, we parked her SUV and began our long on-foot journey westward.

Before us was a landscape fit for 1964's *Woman of the Dunes* if sun-cracked mud had replaced the banks of sand. Empty and barren, the region fit the bill for solitude, bordered by an unending expanse of sagebrush and tumbleweeds. We walked, and we walked, and our minds wandered. I thought of *The Little Prince* as the horizon receded behind mirage: "One sits down on a desert sand dune, sees nothing, hears nothing," Antoine de Saint-Exupéry writes. "Yet through the silence something throbs, and gleams."

Water, I thought. Or maybe a talc block? Boojum tree bark? On bad days, our feet were the thing that throbbed and gleamed with fresh-stained blood.

We arrived deep, deep in the underworld, in a tunnel of pea-sized gravel and emerald leaves. Spiny tridents of yucca emerged from islands of rock. Beyond, if you looked closely, cliffs were hidden behind vegetative blankets of ferns, grasses, and trees. Within them, caverns were covered with mounds of feather tufts, owl pellets, and splinters of rabbit bone, their walls natural mosaics of prismatic cobble, all earth-toned with apologies to salmon-red. Around the corner was their counterpart in gray-scale: ovate, ebony stones, so smooth and dark you could watch your reflection pass over them like a house of mirrors.

Other underworlds, I find, share human geographies: lungs that expel warm, face-blasting pockets of air, a stomach that digests stone with carbonic acid, and blood-pumping tunnels that lead straight to the heart—an unspoken but unanimously agreed upon center place. But this landscape was distinctly inhuman, as if formed within a mollusk's intimate, scalloped shadows—a knife-edged sky that tasted like ocean.

We soon found ancient paintings near the canyon floor: frightening characters adorned with jagged teeth and empty eyes. With outstretched hands, they snatched birds by the wings, their heads cocked backward as if to cackle at their nefarious deeds. Surrounding them were insects, one perhaps a cricket or grasshopper, others more ambiguous and mystical with long spindling legs and antennae.

Just a few feet from the paintings, the tail, armor, and hip of an ankylosaur were embedded waist-high in the side of the alcove. The bones were weathered and purplish, the only memory of its form deposited over one hundred million years ago when this desert held lakes, swamps, and rivers. With a clubbed tail and a fierce body of armor, ankylosaurs once rumbled through this region like bony tanks. Now, this Cretaceous beast was fossilized in a gravelly cement. I had the feeling that we, too, were becoming stratified, that we slithered through bedrock and entered a relic world unseen.

—

Once, I traveled to this place with my two dogs. One, a gluttonous chocolate lab and runt of the litter grown into a chestnut-colored butterball. The other, a blue heeler rescue with deep-set herding instincts, walking with one eye turned to be certain I followed.

I was young and ready for a bold and noble adventure, the likes of which Otto Lidenbrock had surely known in his journey to the center of the earth. My parents lingered behind, respecting my need to experience solitude when the weather precluded my hiking-from-house escapades. They gave me a phone and a red whistle, should I need them.

I sauntered in greedily, taking every second to enjoy my untimely pleasures. I sniffed the rich tang of piñon sap and gently caressed the topography of spiny claret cups. I tasted piñon nuts, now hardened and dried, and spat them back out. I placed my bare hands against rocks, feeling the residual warmth of the sun now below the horizon. When all else was finished, I waited on the rim, examining out-of-reach alcoves across the canyon. Within moments, a bundle of frost-white feathers emerged from a nest. *There.* A great horned owlet, wings just slightly opened, her eyelids flickering over an eclipse of yellow iris.

With the burn of frostnip coursing through my fingers, I cinched my balaclava, squinted my eyes, and balled my fists into pant pockets. I walked farther than they wanted. I always did. There is something of the unknown that must lower inhibition—a stimulant-by-curiosity sort of deal. In my sober, Mormon-boy mind, there was little difference between wanderlust and drunken stupor. And here I was, black-out drunk with nothing short of insatiable snoopiness.

I found the alcove as snow started to fall. After crawling inside, I tightened the dogs' winter coats and turned to find figures standing behind me: haunting beings, painted in shadows, eyes still and vacant. A row of long-eared characters marched below in the light of my headlamp, not much longer than my fingernails, with pursed little snouts looking for mischief. Near them, mystical beings held long, thin lines like proboscises, with two head appendages that oft blurred the line between horn and antennae. I moved closer to them on my knees, holding back tears, overcome by these beings delivered like a divine message.

For years after this encounter, I had a reoccurring dream. There were owl-eyed figures with buggish claws. They were circumnavigated by painted, shaggy birds that swiveled through the air and dived with synched-tight wings. Insects scattered around, crawling through huecos tunneled deep in bedrock. As the dream continued, a stabbing pain entered in my shoulder and worked its way down my body—neck, back, arms, abdomen, and into my scar tissue. When the pain became too much to bear, it progressed into the landscape, where it consumed much. First, the bones. *Gone.* Then the cliffs. *Gone.* Then the sky. *Gone.* With only the alcove and I remaining, I watched the paintings crumble from the cliff in a million blood-red pieces. It took what it knew I needed. And then, when my body was taken from this world, there was only the white plane, a dull hum sounding in the empty infinite. I was suddenly transported to a temple, the Manti Temple, where my family was sealed together. In a white room, beneath a towering glass chandelier, there was silence. Silence was all that was left of me.

—

When I left the church, I came back to this canyon accompanied by Diane, rescinding my baptism in this underworld confessional. I felt like shouting it, making a proclamation to the ether, but only the letter would be necessary. A few weeks later, despite the best efforts of our stake president to convince me otherwise, I received a response:

Dear Brother Bailey:

This letter is to notify you that, in accordance with your request, your name has been removed from the membership records of The Church of Jesus Christ of Latter-day Saints.

Should you desire to become a member of the Church in the future, the local bishop or branch president in your area will be happy to help you.

Sincerely,

Manager, Confidential Records

Market Sojourn

Dear Jonathan,

I am now talking to myself. Great. It's okay. I'm just having a panic attack. Let me give me some advice: walk to the wine shelf casually and place back that bottle of Chardonnay. Gently. Don't drop it. I am in the middle of a grocery store and, given my glassy stare, people are going to think I'm either underage or planning to steal it. A man has already asked if I am feeling ill. I told him no, but I may well pass out.

Outside, a woman spins an advertisement for affordable housing. The streetlights blink red and green. Horns honk, people chatter, and the store's background music cuts through my skull like the neighbor kid's kazoo. There are rows of chocolate, supplement pills, shampoo bottles, something called Damiana all vying for my attention. Choices. Noises. Colors. Pay attention, people need to get through. Now look away. Decide, pick something, move forward. Socialize. Everything is out of control. My delicate senses make me feel feverish, so I stumble out of the store empty-handed and dizzy.

A homeless man walks up to me and begs for money. I ignore him but feel bad when his expression bears discontent. I turn to apologize but the street spins and wobbles. I can't speak. A college student—who appeared from God knows where—asks if I am registered to vote in the state of Arizona. I act like I don't hear him, so he steps out in front of me. "Real mature. Answer me!" he yells, pouting his face. I turn around and keep walking . . . and he keeps shouting. Dogs bark, a billboard flickers, the sweet pecks of a Gila woodpecker thump like a jackhammer through the palo verdes. There are sirens, construction alarms. A policeman asks accusing questions, certain I must be publicly intoxicated. I gesture a reply that must have satisfied him, as I am not handcuffed against his Chevrolet. I try to cross the street with cars hissing through my occipital lobe and very nearly get plowed by a blue SUV I overlooked, somehow, even though I've been standing on this sidewalk for what seems like an eternity.

I walk until I find a patch of grass and close my knees tightly against my chest, rubbing my palms into the corner of my eye sockets, soothed temporarily by the sensory blackout. I am bothered by this city. I want to be anywhere else. Looking toward the Tucson Mountains, I wonder how long I could survive in the Sonoran Desert until I lost a watering hole, or missed too many dinners, and became one of those mummified bodies they show in documentaries—sunbaked into a time capsule and preserved for thousands of years. Maybe a future archaeologist will find some nearly invisible indication of stress buried in my bones. They will assume I was being hunted or sacrificed and, come to think of it, it often feels that way. I am in a society designed for someone else—for the neurological majority—and their needs and norms are hardwired to make me feel alert and over-stimulated.

I stay here, beneath ornamental oranges, in this crescent of manufactured wild until my pulse vacates my eardrums. White-winged doves puff their chests on the cornice of a nearby building, cooing tenderly to the yellowing dusk. Dark-eyed juncos pluck fat worms from underneath the lawn, hopping softly in a stirring breeze. A black-tailed gnatcatcher flies down to a low branch, looking like a round sphere in his white-chested feathers, paired with the most adorable, beady-black eyes I've ever seen.

He cheeps sweetly, nearly a squeak, freeing me from this sensory hangover. And I realize, then, that I love birds. This thought nearly brings me to tears. A love that could break me. I stare at them huddling in this tiny refuge and want them to live forever, be happy always, and never struggle. Do humans bother them too? The noises? The advertisements? The pace of everything? I rattle through my questions, but then they look up, gulping down their yellow grubs, and tilt their heads in confusion.

They fly off in unison as if to answer my questions, spooked by a young couple entering the field with a portable speaker. The pair pull down their sunglasses and string a hammock between the trees, smothering their faces with sunscreen. With nowhere else to go, I take the long journey home and write this, because that is all I can do. I write as if I had those wings.

Uncomfortable

The sign reads *Feld Davis Pocket Park*, "pocket" because it occupies just a single lot. I am in this speck of vegetation in a wide, *wide* city, zooming out on my cell phone map to find more buildings, empty lots, gravel and grass to subdue the native vegetation with urban comforts. Today is my birthday and I'm experiencing a distinct type of depression I know with annual familiarity. There is something about turning a year that forces me to cross-examine every dried, desiccated seed of hope. I cling to a desire that they will sprout, knowing full well many are too old, too damaged. They are weathered and sunbaked, darkened into that dormant polish that says *I am no longer viable*. I soak it like an old habit until it inevitably breaks, holding its fragments between my fingers. But this hope feels most uninhabitable, gritty like seed long abandoned.

On a telephone pole perches a red-tailed hawk. A female. She unfolds her copper wings, flashing her primary feathers. I struggle to focus on her because, today, I am reckoning with a deeper truth. My sexuality is one obstacle. My disabilities, another. Together, somehow, they form the pith of my yearly troubles: my humanity. There is an irony here, in this life I have chosen, because animals have stolen my spirit, yet I rarely work with them in a professional capacity. The reason is simple: animals break me like a ceremonial water jug. I cannot stick a lens in their face and come home unshattered, as if the act gathered some elusive loot. I become so sensitive to their anxieties, I truly come to fear myself. It is a sensation of crawling out of my skin, seeing the world with rodent-fixed senses, and finding some lanky hominid in my crosshairs celebrating his birthday. Somewhere in those bisque-colored eyes, I know its fear, because I fear me, too. Humanity leaves so much heartache and destruction, yet every sad documentary of dead polar bears and burning forests and graveyards of stricken amphibians does not do enough to persuade humanity's political willpower. As climate change ravages human and animal communities, many *will* die while someone, likely a sickeningly wealthy someone, picks their teeth with talons of the last hawk. I yield to that same desperation, to that feeling of helplessness that prevents us from acting meaningfully. I am angry. I am afraid for a future I may not have. I feel defeated in the face of so much death, so much extinction. I know it will only get worse. I didn't ask to be born. So often I can no longer discern if these feelings of disconnection come from my psychology or the flawed human world the hawk and I inhabit.

But there is something else in our shared discomforts. Being atypical—whatever that may mean—makes me panicked in this neurotypical world. My eyes dart. I try my damnedest to travel unseen. At its worst, my anxiety has been described by police officers and paranoid neighbors as downright suspicious. I sense the physical and mental paths traveled by animals because I must walk them, too. I know the route with the least grinding traffic, the backroads where I won't be touched by wayfaring solicitors. I pass homeless people in culverts, concealing themselves in trash deposited by flash floods, trying to become unseen. I know where I can find this solitude, only to discover animals staring back, wondering what the fuck I'm doing in their slivered ecosystems. What hurts most is this realization: I am an invasive species, even in my own communities, even in this wildness in which I feel most at peace. Perhaps I am being too pessimistic.

Perhaps it is the birthday depression. Perhaps I should crinkle this page and surrender to the narrative that society wants from me—an overcoming. But my life is not Plato's cave and my words are not a slow waltz into sunlight. Sometimes everything still hurts. Sometimes it bleeds. Sometimes I can't remember if I want to be seen or invisible and hide in obscurity. Sometimes there is no arc to a story and all power rests in telling the truth.

Honestly, I feel like a fish out of water, given drop by drop to survive, but never enough to be sufficiently alive. I wait on this sun-dried embankment, telling stories I am told to tell, being the person I am told to be, but slowly suffocating. I long for a sea too far, too salty for my freshwater lungs. There comes a time, I find, when temporary relief feels indistinguishable from torture, delaying the inevitable and prolonging the suffering. The hawk and I have no choice but to adapt to this changing world, but neither of us can do it fast enough.

I follow a woman through reeds
on all fours, light glinting
on cottonwood seeds.
Water drips into our boots,
in whirls.
We crawl.
Our hands are calloused, burning.
Mud cakes beneath our nails
like blood.
We crawl.
We crawl.
Her hair is black, sooty, like roots
beneath the water.
I reach to grab it, knowing
it is moss. Knowing it will stretch
and break
in skinny strands. Between my fingers,
I wrap her hair, around my body,
against my armpits,
to join our warmths.
We crawl.

Her hands meet the dirt, and she digs
in a frenzy, fingers bleeding
in deep pools.

Holes emerge beneath her hands
and we creep inside,
where the air is sharp, choking,
like water.

Roots shrivel beneath our toes, reaching
the surface, a climbing death.
So much death. It is hot,
then cold. So cold.
Hurricanes writhe over the
above world, taking everything
but this refuge. Bodies
pile. Mass graves. Blood is
water. Water is blood.
We engorge
ourselves on both.

No earth
for saving.
No life
to perish.
Everything has
passed from this plane
of being,
like water.

"So you've left the church," my father says, his lips quivering to hold back tears. "I found your resignation letter in the mailbox."

"Dad . . ."

"It breaks my heart. Our family, we were sealed together. We went to the temple and made a commitment."

"I know."

"Do you even believe in God anymore?"

"No, I don't."

"So, we have no purpose? All this creation just to die. Then, nothing? A black pit of despair? That's it. Is that what you believe?"

"I don't know. That's a theory, one based on observations and, to be fair, a healthy dose of interpretation. There's still a lot we don't fully understand."

"Why are we here, then? We must have purpose. Heavenly Father gives us purpose."

"Dad, we are surrounded with purpose. Remember our peach trees? We planted them. We nurture them. Then, robins came down and they feasted until they could hardly lift their chubby little bellies off the ground. I know they give you head-aches, but *that's* purpose. We live in everything that has crossed our path. We are the reason they go home with full stomachs and a smile in their hearts. Not to mention our ponderosas. They started as a single sapling, that little tree Jessica won at the

Arbor Day art contest. Now, several reach the sky, with generations of owlets among their progeny. We can't put a foot on the grass without changing the world—hopefully for the better. It is a sacred duty to be of this planet with no greater purpose than to have obligations to it."

"Jonathan, earthly life is a small part of our spiritual lives. We prepare—in some ways—to die. What about family? What about death? What do you *want* to happen?"

"I have tried my best to come to terms with anything, including my own uncertainty. I guess I hope death is like shale. Shale is made of a lot of tiny fragments of minerals—primarily clay, some quartz, calcite—that become cemented together by water, assuming it has the right chemicals. Eventually, the shale falls, or succumbs to other erosive forces, and there comes a time when the shale is no more. But all the things that make shale 'shale' persist, just not together, not as an entity. Some minerals stay in place—perhaps nourishing our garden unbeknownst to us— while the wind takes other minerals from clay and brings them to other communities of life. We are also made up of a lot of 'stuff.' A lot of living stuff. Whatever consciousness is—and I'm afraid no theory satisfies my curiosity—I hope it is something like shale, and that we don't become nothing, we become more. I hope we shatter."

"So you're saying that you want us to turn to dust?"

"No, I'm saying that I want to spend the rest of time as a part of the earth—all of it—not just as a resident upon it."

Many years ago, I met a tarantula during a trance. Her front legs were upraised, flickering in golden light. With each conscious breath, I observed a marked shift in color, rippling in waves of hue like clockwork: royal blues, indigo, veering to deep crimson, and back again. She positioned her body readily among the rocks but still timid, coiled back.

Her blackness concealed her outline as she prowled the shadowed edges of the vision, light split through her hairs into inscrutable shapes and luminous polychromes as if she wore needles of abalone shell through her abdomen. *Hypnotic.* She stopped and turned to face me briefly, suspended but a few inches from my face. *But her eyes.* Her eyes glistened obsidian behind the hairs on her pedipalps, the arm-like appendages in front of her body. I felt all eight eyes penetrating, thinking, nudging ever closer to curiosity. As I breathed out, she scampered back into the underworld, the inner dens of thought.

Inhale.

Raindrops strike the rocks methodically, my breath now in sync with their rhythm. My guide was wilderness and the thoughtful intake of air. No psychoactive substances were needed, simply a commitment to the process. On the edge of sleep, hallucinations are produced by a drifting consciousness. I am forced back to physical awareness by external stimuli. Rinse and repeat, the cycle continues. Strands of thought and sleep are woven together, a memory is borne from consciousness.

I first turned to meditation to cope with anxiety, depression, and sensory sensitivities. As I trained longer, and in stranger places, with even more obscure intentions, I used it to deeply experience my surroundings. I now not only recognize the sound of a coyote's yowl, but also the sensation it triggers while detached from my body. The call enters through my scalp like a sudden burst of electricity, traveling through the spine and toward the tips of my fingers. My shoulders instinctively pull backward as the tingling travels over my skin, eventually vacating through the palms of my hands.

And exhale.

Meditation is like onset blindness while discovering the landscape through new senses. I have come to recognize the distinctive *shuck shuck* of the Sonoran collared lizard marching in the leaves, knowing if it were any larger, or any smaller, or if its tail-to-body ratio was swapped, the noises it produced would change with it. I sometimes *feel* a sense of displacement while Huachuca Mountain scorpions scramble beneath the cobblestones, their legs scraping against the inner soil like little fingernails. Awareness is like a good field guide, reintroducing you to familiar spaces.

Inhale.

When I meditate in the desert, I feel connected, as if flora and fauna have tapped into this knowing. I like to imagine distant jaguars chewing on branches of yagé, also known as ayahuasca, a hallucinogenic plant in South America with verdant green foliage. The psychological effects are not well understood in jaguars, but they can be seen behaving more like kittens after consuming the plant. In humans, ayahuasca is said to have varying results, depending largely on the "set and setting"—the predetermined intention of the trip and the environment in which it is occurring. Like many psychoactive (mind-affecting) substances, DMT, the chemical contained within ayahuasca, is reported to bring a sense of connectivity with the natural world.

Many also experience ego death—an experience that dissolves the stuff "you" are made of, like your name, family, belongings, or sense of self. While only scarcely similar to the experiences of meditation, yagé shares these sensations of erosion and togetherness.*

And exhale.

A raindrop patters off the giant trumpeting flowers of *Datura wrightii*, or sacred datura, a member of the nightshade family along with the likes of peppers and tomatoes. At night, its bone-white flowers unfurl, ready to be pollinated by hawkmoths (hence one of its poetic common names, the moonflower).

All parts of sacred datura are rich with deadly poisons, containing alkaloids like scopolamine, hyoscyamine, and atropine that can impact the nervous system. The plant is a powerful hallucinogen used by Indigenous people. In some communities, datura is believed to be a dangerous gateway to the spirit world, allowing shamans to communicate with the deceased or the spirits responsible for rainfall or game animals. Sometimes it made them crazy. Some of these individuals have given their lives to the plant, overcome in its deadly embrace, or lost in a psychotic break.

Inhale.

When cannabis was legalized in Arizona, I bought a bag of edibles with the intention of relieving the most resistant anxiety patterns, to promising success. I took a bag of gummies with me to the Dragoon Mountains to sleep through the night. This was when I learned the importance of "settling," the process by which the sugar coating—containing the psychoactive compound THC—settles to the bottom of the bag.

That was an interesting evening.

---

* 5-MeO-DMT is also sourced from Sonoran Desert toad (Incilius alvarius) toxins, which is dangerous, highly unethical, and stresses toad populations toward extinction. All DMT is a controlled substance under federal law.

The trees warped into a tunnel as I walked, distracted by thoughts of jackals and the inevitable swaying of bodily limbs that follows a high dose of cannabis. I wasn't certain I could walk at all. The Milky Way was a literal river with cobble and star-flecks of mica. I laid in my tent and watched it rise and flow through the trees. My perception was sharp. Nothing escaped my notice. Except where I was. Or who I was. Or why I was here. Which direction was up, anyway? Music was ineffably more magical, every note a sounding board ripping open my heart and leaving it out to bleed. Somewhere, I could taste the warmth of a campfire on the tip of my tongue, licking my lips at its dryness. I decided to leave for my tent to sleep it out. My camping companion came to me and placed her hand on my shoulder. *Goodnight, Jonathan.* I felt every finger as an exchange of heat and softness. I felt it tingle deeply in my skin. People danced around us with lightsabers and ghoulish masks which—much to my surprise—was not a hallucination.

Fucking LARPers.

I intersected with a part of my being that I didn't know existed that night, one who can accept bad things and carry them as a gift. The process of a high can be something like the reconciliation of trauma, with peaks of discomfort that ebb and drift onward when you learn to accept them.

I woke up in the middle of the night to a pool of sweat.

But the shores of my mind felt cleaner. For *days*.

Inhale.

I seek healing and connection in my life. In meditation, grounding is an important technique to maintain both. It requires feeling the earth beneath your hands and feet, sensing the points of contact with your surroundings. Of equal significance is letting go of that connection, allowing the mind to wander freely. Like our experiences of wild places, we must flow with the push and pull of forces beyond control. I am not here to repress my thoughts, feelings, or the processes of wilderness, simply to observe them.

I am here to let go.

And exhale.

Ten miles from Ferron lived my maternal grandmother, Ruth. I remember driving up to her cottage-like trailer with chalk-white paint and red trim, tucked behind a pavilion where we watched hummingbirds rejoice in flowers and sugar water. A joyful woman of few words, she walked outside as we approached, waiting to embrace me into her warm but firm arms.

Although her house was in a sparsely populated desert, I imagined it set in mountainous terrain. Several pine trees surrounded the fence-lined entry, bordered by potted apricot-colored flowers. In the back, birch trees were planted between rocks "visiting"—she would say—from open spaces: agates, shales, and our favorite, sandstone. If the rocks could not find a home in her garden, they were given space on pavilion tables, accompanied by an assortment of marine fossils. She was, among many things, a connoisseur of wonder, reminding me that the area's semiarid deserts were once a shallow inland sea.

There were two more trough-like planters behind her house where she kept wildflowers transplanted from many places. Her prize was a cobalt penstemon passed down from my great-great-uncle, Hyrum, who brought it from the Manti hills behind the Wasatch Mountains. The species was not rare or particularly unusual, but it was descended from seeds clutched in his weathered, desert-loving hands. After losing three of her daughters, Ruth seemed to find reassurance in safeguarding the memory of others, including her grandfather, David, who became blind after he escaped from the Mexican Revolution. Despite his condition, he was a skilled carver and rug-weaver, sensing the tingle of symmetry and beauty beneath his calloused fingers. He soon found opportunities to teach the sighted and delighted in the ability to better their lives. He told Ruth that adversity was a gift that taught him to see truth in life's lessons. Contentment through hardship.

—

The last time I entered Ruth's house was also the first time she truly saw me. I brought Aaron, but the display of affection wasn't needed. She knew I was gay. She was warm, understanding. We sat against one of her blankets and reflected on the creatures we both cherished, and the people we both loved.

A few months later, I received a phone call and knew instantly that Ruth had passed from this world. I didn't answer the phone. Instead, I walked. I walked through a river, over sandstone, past dragonflies, beneath cottonwoods that seemed strangely larger than they should. I felt her everywhere and nowhere, her presence and her absence, and then—when the moment came—I let her go.

I did not cry. I would miss her, of course, but it felt that fate had fallen where it fitted. She met with most everyone in the family, greeted her newest great-granddaughter, and, personally, I was given the gift of parting with her truthfully. One evening shortly thereafter, she walked in the front door and her heart stopped—I wonder if from growing too large.

Now, five years after her death, I see her face in a black-and-white photograph when she was but a young adult. She is holding a pistol with a sly grin that speaks to just how out of character she must feel using it. Through uniform census records, obituaries, testimonies of hardship and faith, this photograph is *my* heritage—a sly grin in the face of adversity, holding a firearm for no other reason—I imagine—than to defy expectation.

"Memory is persistence—to exist is to remember why one exists . . ." I write in *The Greater San Rafael Swell.* "Like the cascading song of the canyon wren from the onset of spring, I sense that it is the remembrance of our 'songs,' our histories, that revitalizes us as a species."

People like Ruth gave me the gift of songs free of cages too small and solitary. I cherish it. I have returned to nests long forgotten, to explain why I am here, and to resolve everything from my height to my predisposition for shoddy eyes. I love them, honor them, and find kinship in family trees. But old nests are meant to be visited, not lived in. To look too keenly upon heritage is to become *Mimus polyglottos,* a mockingbird—a borrower of songs. Frankly, I am no mockingbird. Neither was Ruth. I want to speak freely of the life I have lived, reclaim the parts of myself taken from me. I want to understand and even respect my culture without surrendering to it, because the memory I seek is tenderness, not mimicry.

Buhle

By January 1, 2021, it will have been ten years since I came out. Many of my friends and family are ill with COVID-19. The less fortunate look for food, employment, for family who passed in unsettling white rooms. But I am transfixed by an owl. She is a tiny, fist-sized ball of fluff, asleep in a Christmas wreath constructed of red chile peppers. I find her snuggled against a corn husk ribbon, following my movements without flicking her eyes open.

My friend Gregory has named her Buhle.

She is the color of oak bark, with dark feather bands indistinguishable from shadows. She is now but a few feet away, breathing softly, her beak cinched tight against her chest. I think of her amber eyes but cannot see them. There is stillness in her slumber that feels prescient.

Vaccines are near.

An election is over.

Ten years. Six of those have been spent with Aaron. I am now seven hundred miles away from Ferron, writing beneath storm clouds from the western Pacific. Winds have picked up. Rain falls briefly. There is unresolve in the air, but it does not expel its calmness. Somehow, and I can't explain it, I *feel* turquoise. The color is in my lungs, humid air from distant gulfs. I imagine it in the Colorado River as it moves south, bridging me between Sonora and the Swell. I see it in the swimming pools luminous against sandy stucco walls. It is a color of transition, neither grief nor tranquility. Perhaps it is the color of movement.

I have never been this close to an owl and I feel breathless. She is wild and beautiful, an adult in the genus *Megascops*. A western screech owl. Her eyes squint open, and then she does something that my ornithologist friends would very much doubt: she smiles. Her whole face rises and compresses with the expression, then she exhales and falls gently back to sleep. I take it as a sign to tiptoe out and leave her resting peacefully.

I have a selfish desire I must confess. I wish to know the shape of her owl dreams—the touch of moonlight against feathers, the crinkle of small rodent feet beneath desert scrub, an adjustment of the iris that quells darkness in an instant. I start to wonder if these dreams are hers or my own. I resolve that these are dreams we must share.

I arrive back home and do something drastic. I pierce both ears and insert earrings of abalone, jet, coral, and turquoise. They are round, Zuni crafted, split in mosaics shaped into mesas viewed from afar. I cut my hair, dye it blue, and tattoo my skin with sacred datura. Outside, the rain still falls. Red clay succumbs to azure pools. I feel I can no longer bear to live under expectations that are not my own. I am seven hundred miles away, and out of reach of everyone but myself and my beloved. This red clay becomes turquoise. I take this color because I, too, am trying to move on.

If you didn't take the time to know me, I may not seem like a text-book minority. I have blond hair, blue eyes, and, perhaps above all, I am a white male. Still, at times, it feels as if I couldn't be more different than the community from which I grew up. I am, among many things, an ex-Mormon, gay, and a staunch advocate for conservation and the climate. I also struggle with mental health. Despite my otherness, in over two decades of living in rural Utah, I was always able to find people who chose to treat me with dignity and respect. It just required some searching. I think of my English teacher, Diane, who dared to question what makes a family, and gave me the courage to have an uncomfortable conversation about the suicide rates among LGBTQ+ Mormon youth among my classmates. Taci, one of the few students who stood with me, still checks on me. Jim Keele, a dear belated friend and former teacher, let me stay in his office whenever demons—internal and external—seemed to overwhelm. I have watched my parents grow as individuals, becoming healthier, happier, and supportive people. For their sake, I hope they find peace. I have also seen Mormon elders praying for my success, their heads bowed in a corner beneath my exhibits. *Small acts matter.* The relationships I have shared, both human and wild, save lives and spirits.

This community, small but with a spacious heart, has laid a solid foundation for how I lead my life and how I envision my American identity: one that is collaborative, open, forgiving, and unconditionally kind. At the end of the day, I hope we are still more than "us vs them," and it is time for all of us to come together, in person, beyond our screens, and preferably in wild spaces.

Wilderness teaches that diversity is not only normal but celebrated. Flora and fauna have evolved a vast range of strategies to survive in habitats ranging from the most arid to humid pockets of water. Caught between two seemingly irreconcilable positions, these species are still joined by desert soils, and by a warming climate that may well impact their livelihoods. They need not adapt to each other, forcing one into a space where it is unfit to survive, but must exist in balance, joining to endure their hardships together. How can we learn from them to better our communities rife with such vitriol and division?

Deep down, humans are still animals—or as my friend R. E. Burrillo would say: "squishy animals"—and we still have fears and emotions that are, like the coyote gourd, anachronisms, adaptations for ways of life that have fallen to the wayside in our industrialized world. But these adaptations are important. We still need to feel supported. We need fresh air. We need to believe our work and contributions matter. We need close family and friendships. In part, depression and anxiety are not always *just* mental illnesses but responses to these anachronisms, telling us to find friends and seek support because, throughout human history, people who lived in tight, caring, and ecologically responsible communities *survived*. Those communities are increasingly rare in our chaotic present. Most of us have strayed so far from our birth planet that clean air, open space, and empathy for non-human beings are foreign concepts. But our species evolved over millions of years in wild spaces and with loving companions, becoming reliant both emotionally and physically on the land and on each other. That severance does not go without heavy consequences.

Society still has choices for humanity. We can still fight climate change. We can still find a healthier, more nurturing way to live. We can reconnect with our planet in the ways we are able, be it a city park of native species, our garden ecosystems, in true wilderness, or through the warmth of our home windows. It need not look the same for everyone. We can still connect with our political opposites, recognize their humanity, and pave a better, kinder future. We can even connect with ourselves, no matter our age, and discover inner truths. We need only follow in the footsteps of wilderness, with wise teachers ranging from the smallest of lives to the largest, and in more colors and shapes than you can imagine. Perhaps my story can serve as a guide, reintroducing the special worlds we have lost, both inside and outside, within our communities and beyond.

acknowledgments

The people who helped bring this project to life are far too numerous to name individually, but include (in alphabetical order): Archaeology Southwest and their wonderful employees for generous and friendly support; Gregory Anderson for giving me the opportunity to meet Buhle; Kathleen Bader for support and being one of the kindest people I know; Connie Barlow for sending me so much information on evolutionary anachronisms; the Bailey family for countless reasons; Nina Bowen for always being kind and supportive; R. E. Burrillo for reviewing drafts and for constant feedback; Diane Carter for providing nurturing spaces and reviewing the manuscript; Paul Christiansen for reviewing poems; Alan Cressler for many travels and for allowing me to tap into his vast knowledge; Keeley Criswell and David Schwartz for reviewing drafts and offering advice; Jim Dabakis for being a source of much kindness and bottomless support; Kevin Dahl for thoughtful conversations and information on seeds; Paul Davidson for wonderful moss conversations; William Doelle for his incredible generosity; Eric Eaton for help with tarantula hawks; Aaron Goldtooth for many memories and years of companionship; Camille Gonzalez for reviewing material and providing advice; Donald Grayson for giving me so much information on megafauna and evolutionary anachronisms; Ryan Hermansen for photo assistance and travels; Alexander Garvey Holbrook for providing detailed feedback and a fresh pair of eyes; Troy Honanie Jr. for valued conversations and feedback; Matt Jarvis for being an incredible human and an incredible friend; Olivia Juarez for feedback; John Kartesz for creating the BONAP database which proved truly priceless; Jim Keele for many wonderful travels; Katie Lee for always encouraging my work; Julie Alma Lindholm for so much support and friendship; Connie Massingale for many stories shared and canyons traveled; Kari McWest for valued help on scorpions; Dan Millis for so much information on the borderlands; Lorraine Bailey-Moreland for being truly family; Diane Orr for deep, heartfelt and thought-provoking conversations and years of joining me in the field to protect the places we cherish; Steven Platt for information on peccaries and the coyote gourd; the Salt Lake Tribune for brief segments that have been republished; Kate Sarther for so much support and being another one of the kindest people I know; Al Schneider for his wonderful online resources and for generously providing me with a rare copy of *A Utah Flora*; Morgan Sjogren for thoughtful conversations and advice; Southern Utah Wilderness Alliance for kind and generous support; Stephen Strom for intensively reviewing my material and offering generous connections that made sections of this work possible; Robert Villa for the forward and wondrous conversations; Stanley Welsh for letting me tap into his vast flora knowledge; Jade Yazzie for transportation; and many others.

works cited

"Autism Spectrum Disorder," National Institute of Mental Health, last revised March 2018, https://www.nimh.nih.gov/health/topics/autism-spectrum-disorders-asd.

Bagemihl, Bruce. *Biological Exuberance: Animal Homosexuality and Natural Diversity*. New York: St. Martin's Press, 1999.

Coyote, Ivan and Rae Spoon. *Gender Failure*. Vancouver: Arsenal Pulp Press, 2014.

de Saint-Exupéry, Antoine. *The Little Prince*. New York: Reynal & Hitchcock, April 1943.

Goldtooth, Frank. "In the Beginning: A Navaho Creation Myth." By Stanley A Fishler. Anthropological Papers, Department of Anthropology, University of Utah No. 13, January 1953. *http://www.sacred-texts.com/nam/nav/itb/index.htm*.

Granger, Max. "The Border Patrol is Leaving People to Die." *High Country News*, February 2021.

Kimmerer, Robin Wall. *Braiding Sweetgrass: Indigenous Wisdom, Scientific Knowledge, and the Teachings of Plants*. Minneapolis: Milkweed Editions, 2013.

Loeffler, Jack, "Listening to Our Sibling Deserts: Restoring Indigenous Mindfulness," in *The Nature of Desert Nature*, edited by Gary Paul Nabhan. Tucson: University of Arizona Press, 2020.

Meloy, Ellen. *The Anthropology of Turquoise: Reflections on Desert, Stone, Sea, and Sky*. New York: Vintage, 2002.

Monson, Thomas S. "We Need Pioneers Today." *Ensign*, July 2013.

Oaks, Dallin H. "Same-Gender Attraction." Referencing Book of Mormon, 2 Nephi 2:27-29. *Ensign*, March 1996.

Obergefell v. Hodges, No. 14-556, June 26, 2015.

O'Keeffe, Georgia. *From the Faraway, Nearby*. 1937. Oil on canvas, 36 × 40 1/8 in. (91.4 × 101.9 cm), The Met Fifth Avenue, New York, https://www.metmuseum.org/art/collection/search/489064.

Packer, Boyd K. "To Young Men Only." Sermon at the 146th Semiannual General Conference of the Church of Jesus Christ of Latter-day Saints on October 2, 1976.

Santayana, George. *The Life of Reason*. Buffalo: Prometheus, 1998.

Strom, Stephen E. and Jonathan T. Bailey. *The Greater San Rafael Swell: Honoring Tradition and Preserving Storied Lands*. Tucson: University of Arizona Press, 2022.

Thoreau, Henry David. "Walking." *The Atlantic*, June 1862.

Tosa, Paul in *Rock Art: A Vision of a Vanishing Cultural Landscape* by Jonathan T. Bailey. Denver: Johnson Books, 2019.

further reading and resources

American Pleistocene & Ice Age

Grayson, Donald. *Giant Sloths and Sabertooth Cats: Extinct Mammals and the Archaeology of the Ice Age Great Basin.* Salt Lake City: University of Utah Press, 2016.

Childs, Craig. *Atlas of a Lost World: Travels in Ice Age America.* New York: Vintage, 2019.

MacPhee, Ross D. and Peter Schouten. *End of the Megafauna: The Fate of the World's Hugest, Fiercest, and Strangest Animals.* New York: W. W. Norton, 2018.

Damselflies & Dragonflies

Bailowitz, Richard. *Field Guide to the Damselflies and Dragonflies of Arizona and Sonora.* Tucson: Nova Granada Publications, 2015.

Plants, General

Kimmerer, Robin Wall. *Braiding Sweetgrass: Indigenous Wisdom, Scientific Knowledge, and the Teachings of Plants.* Minneapolis: Milkweed Editions, 2013.

Kimmerer, Robin Wall. *Gathering Moss: A Natural and Cultural History of Mosses.* Corvallis: Oregon State University Press, 2003.

Plants, Identification

Welsh, Stanley. *A Utah Flora.* Provo: Monte L Bean Life Science Museum, 2003.

BONAP, http://bonap.org.

Wildflowers, Ferns, and Trees of Colorado, New Mexico, Arizona, and Utah, https://www.swcoloradowildflowers.com.

Plants, Evolutionary Anachronisms

Barlow, Connie. *The Ghosts of Evolution: Nonsensical Fruit, Missing Partners, and Other Ecological Anachronisms.* New York: Basic Books, 2000.

Rock Art

Bailey, Jonathan T. *Rock Art: A Vision of a Vanishing Cultural Landscape.* Denver: Johnson Books, 2019.

Schaafsma, Polly. *Indian Rock Art of the Southwest.* Albuquerque: University of New Mexico Press, 1986.

Cole, Sally J. *Legacy on Stone: Rock Art of the Colorado Plateau and Four Corners Region.* Denver: Johnson Books, 1990.

San Rafael Swell

Strom, Stephen E. and Jonathan T. Bailey. *The Greater San Rafael Swell: Honoring Tradition and Preserving Storied Lands.* Tucson: University of Arizona Press, 2022.

Sonoran Desert

Phillips, Steven J. and Patricia Wentworth Comus, ed. *A Natural History of the Sonoran Desert.* Tucson: Arizona-Sonora Desert Museum Press, 2015.

Southwest Archaeology

Burrillo, R. E. *Behind the Bears Ears: Exploring the Cultural and Natural Histories of a Sacred Landscape.* Salt Lake City: Torrey House Press, 2020.

Cordell, Linda S. and Maxine E. McBrinn. *Archaeology of the Southwest.* Oxfordshire: Routledge, 2012.

Lekson, Stephen H. *A Study of Southwestern Archaeology.* Salt Lake City: University of Utah Press, 2018.

about the author

Jonathan T. Bailey is a conservation photographer with a background in cultural resources. Author of the photograph and essay collection *Rock Art: A Vision of a Vanishing Cultural Landscape*, his work has been published in *Archaeology Southwest*, the *Salt Lake Tribune*, *Indian Country Today*, and elsewhere. He lives in Tucson, Arizona.

TORREY HOUSE PRESS

Voices for the Land

The economy is a wholly owned subsidiary of the environment, not the other way around.
　　　　　　—Senator Gaylord Nelson, founder of Earth Day

Torrey House Press publishes books at the intersection of the literary arts and environmental advocacy. THP authors explore the diversity of human experiences with the environment and engage community in conversations about landscape, literature, and the future of our ever-changing planet, inspiring action toward a more just world. We believe that lively, contemporary literature is at the cutting edge of social change. We seek to inform, expand, and reshape the dialogue on environmental justice and stewardship for the human and more-than-human world by elevating literary excellence from diverse voices.

Visit www.torreyhouse.org for reading group discussion guides, author interviews, and more.

As a 501(c)(3) nonprofit publisher, our work is made possible by generous donations from readers like you.

Torrey House Press is supported by Back of Beyond Books, the King's English Bookshop, Maria's Bookshop, the Jeffrey S. & Helen H. Cardon Foundation, the Sam & Diane Stewart Family Foundation, the Barker Foundation, Diana Allison, Klaus Bielefeldt, Laurie Hilyer, Shelby Tisdale, Kirtly Parker Jones, Robert Aagard & Camille Bailey Aagard, Kif Augustine Adams & Stirling Adams, Rose Chilcoat & Mark Franklin, Jerome Cooney & Laura Storjohann, Linc Cornell & Lois Cornell, Susan Cushman & Charlie Quimby, Betsy Gaines Quammen & David Quammen, the Utah Division of Arts & Museums, Utah Humanities, the National Endowment for the Humanities, the National Endowment for the Arts, the Salt Lake City Arts Council, and Salt Lake County Zoo, Arts & Parks. Our thanks to individual donors, members, and the Torrey House Press board of directors for their valued support.

Join the Torrey House Press family and give today at www.torreyhouse.org/give.

"Utah's Emery County maps hard ideological boundaries over some of the harshest landscapes of the arid West. Even so, the stratified cliffs, seeping recesses, and crustal sinks testify of lush and various inhabitations, eon upon eon. Utterly *here*, Bailey confines us to a temporal body untenable and ecstatic, hypersensitized to the play of surface and interior, opacity and revelation, hostility and intimacy. This kind of writing can only emerge from the awful beauty of always-yet-never Home."

—KARIN ANDERSON, author of
Before Us Like a Land of Dreams

"In Bailey's profoundly moving memoir, the diversity of creation illuminates the inner landscape and inspires healing—and wonder. The past is a gift, Bailey says, and this brave journey into the intimate wilderness is another gift. With the clarity and fresh eyes of meditation, we visit the topography of bones, the meaning of the natural world, and the centering of spirit within ourselves, within community, and in our footsteps and vision. In the true meaning of the word: this book is *awesome*."

—GEORGE K. ILSLEY, author of *The Home Stretch:
A Father, a Son, and All the Things They Never Talk About*

"After leaving the church of his childhood, Bailey realized he always had his religion in the power of nature. The desert saved him. Its ability to heal was always his refuge and became more so as he grew older and life under the strictures of the church became unbearable. *When I Was Red Clay* is about loss, gain, and an homage to the western desert country, a place that can be 'unimaginably bewitching.' When you grow up with an appreciation for the natural world, you find wonder and solace in the smallest things. Sometimes it's just the blue sky or fresh air, sometimes it's following in the footsteps of those who've gone before us in this beautiful land. I read with affinity as Bailey described holding and stroking the scales of a nearly drowned lizard. Haven't we all done this type of thing and been moved by it? I haven't read something so beautiful in a long time. I can't stop thinking about it."

—MARYA JOHNSTON, Out West Books